THE ROAD TO
Becoming

Visit the author's blog at jennysimmons.com

The Fuel Music Management Co
110 Mountain Harbour Dr.
Sparta, TN 38583 USA
www.thefuelmusic.com

Edited by Jana Burson of The Burson Agency

Copy-Edited by Anna Floit of The Peacock Quill

Cover Design by Ryan Simmons

Interior Design by Emily Keafer Lambright of Every Little Thing Studio

Author photo taken by Eric Brown Photography, © 2014. All rights reserved.

ISBN-13: 978-0-692-27990-8

First Edition

Printed in the United States of America

THE ROAD TO
Becoming

A journey through seasons of change,
waiting, and finding new *life*.

JENNY SIMMONS

To my SWEET ANNIE:
*If only I could keep you from life's
dead-ends and detours; but then you
would miss the beauty of being lost
and being found. So I will walk every
road, detour, and dead-end with you
for as long as we both shall live.*

To MY MOM, DAD,
SISTERS, IN-LAWS, *and the*
MANY DEAR FRIENDS *who have
walked these long roads with us:
Thank you will never suffice.
You were the streams in our desert.*

To RYAN: *God only knows how
many dead-ends our marriage has
seen, how many detours. But we are
still here, still being lost and found
together, and I am forever grateful.
I love you.*

CONTENTS

Prelude: MANGLEDY-BANGLEDY

◆

Early one morning in the spring of 2011 I woke up in my own bed sweating, afraid, and completely lost. I felt like a piece of driftwood. The mangledy-bangledy kind that gets ripped off a tree during a storm and thrown into a river three counties over, bewildered and broken. I was in a current I could not control. In a river I had never known. Nothing was familiar and *nothing* was going the way I had planned.

I had made *good* plans for my life.

Dreamed up when I was nine years old and the universe was compliant with my every whim. Revised when I was nineteen years old and way smarter than my parents. When I had my existence—*and everyone else's*—all figured out. Revisited after college when all I wanted was a safe road without surprises or detours; a well-laid plan that would tell me my place in the world. But that morning in 2011—as a thirty-one-year-old wife, mom, and successful recording artist, I realized the plans I dreamed up were long gone and I was completely lost.

The worst twelve months of my life were barely behind me. But in that moment, trembling in my own bed and wracked with fear, I would have gone back to that hellish year because at least back then I knew who I was and where I was going. Even if getting there meant enduring a fire, thefts, bankruptcy and complete physical exhaustion. I still knew who I was and where I was going.

But the mornings spent lying in my own bed afraid of the future, unsure of my own name, living in complete lostness? They were breaking me.

With no tears left to cry that particular morning in 2011, I stared the terrifying unknown in the face and knew I was at a crossroad. As I laid there in a daze, dreading the day at hand, it occurred to me that I had spent years encouraging *other* people to live by faith but I had no idea how to live by it myself. I was the kind of girl who wanted faith for other people. Me? I wanted answers, happily-ever-afters and enough control over my life that I did not have to cling to Jesus for my very breath, my very bread. I only wanted religion.

Security has become the drug of choice for religious people who don't really want to live by faith. We naively (arrogantly?) assume there are monuments that we can erect in honor of the steadfast certainties our lives are centered around. Mother! Artist! 401 (k) plan! Philanthropist! Gainfully employed! A path, a plan, a purpose! All monuments. All man-made.

My monuments were well erected. Wife. Mom. Musician. World traveler. Woman of purpose. Woman of faith. My band, Addison Road, was on the radio, traveling around the country on a sold-out tour and had sold nearly 150,000 albums. I was certain we would be making music together well into our nursing home days.

But when those monuments began to crumble, I found myself in the midst of broken dreams with no security and no clue *how* to move forward. Or *where* to move forward. Each new day I woke up with soul paralysis, feeling like a piece of storm-ravaged driftwood.

Being all mangledy-bangledy from a storm is supposed to be a good thing. At least that's what preachers and stoics say. Storms grow you up. Get rid of all the bad stuff in you. Refine you with their holy fire! Apparently some people come out of storms as stronger, shinier, more beautifully refined versions of themselves. And I'm happy for those people. *Kind of.* But that wasn't me. I made it to the other side of the worst year of my life and was, well—worse.

Seasons of hardship can leave us worse for the wear, at least in my experience. Instead of making it to the other side as a better version of ourselves, we can end up bitter, broken, and barely recognizable. Just because one makes it through a hard season and is still standing doesn't mean they have traveled down the life-giving road to becoming something new. It just means their feet still work.

My feet still worked. But nothing else did. I was a mangledy-bangledy mess. That morning in 2011, the Lord whispered something deep inside of my soul. A confirmation of what I long suspected, but fiercely avoided: transformation would only happen if I buried the past and blindly, bravely stepped out into the terrifying, unknown future. That morning the Redeemer of stories invited me into a new kind of journey. It was a long-standing invitation to join the Storyteller on *the road to becoming.* And I finally accepted.

    Three years have passed since that morning in 2011 and I have learned that *the road to becoming* requires much more than just "still standing" after the storm batters and bruises our monuments. It is the journey after the storm, on wobbly knees and tired feet that matters the most. In my own story, after the chapters of Dreaming and Destruction, my life unfolded into an unknown journey marked by distinct seasons that I have come to know as The Burying, The Lostness, The Waiting, and The Becoming. Side by side with the great Storyteller, these distinct stages made up the path that led me to new life.

Perhaps you know what it feels like to dread the day at hand. Your plans have changed, failed, or come to a screeching halt and you are living in the in-between. Not who you were and not yet who you might become. Like driftwood, thrown into a river three counties over, you feel bewildered and broken. Standing—but all kinds of mangledy-bangledy.

Maybe you have asked the same types of questions that I asked. Am I hopeless? Will I ever become something new? And how? When? What? And isn't there a book I can read that will just *give me the freaking answer already?*

Perhaps each new day begins with feeling lost. Another day without a road map. Another prayer whispered or screamed, *How long, oh Lord?*

If nothing more, I share my story to remind you that you are not alone in yours. I am one of many who have gone before you on this road to becoming and surely in time will circle back around once more and pass through the dreaming and destruction, burying, lostness, waiting, and becoming.

There is a moment in each person's journey when leaning into the unknown becomes the only viable pathway to new life. It is at this weighty juncture that a person of faith must ask, "Do I believe the Storyteller knows better than anyone else how to repurpose a piece of driftwood?" If the answer is yes, pack your bags and get ready to follow God into the unknown. The road to becoming is not easy; it is certainly not for the faint of heart. But it is here that we begin to discover new life—*life abundant*—is always, ever among us. Dancing on the horizon.

the
DREAMING
and
DESTRUCTION

1 | MAGNOLIA TREES

❖

When I was a little girl, I had my own magnolia tree. No one else in the world was invited underneath her canopy of waxy citrus leaves. She was all mine. My fortress, my empire.

Under the leaves of a mighty Mississippi magnolia, you can become anyone you want. A pirate or sprite. A wicked witch or withered old man whose only job is to keep the lanterns burning and whisper to weary travelers the secrets of traversing the hidden passageways of the kingdom.

Inside my big laurel I was the boy with a sword and stone—and a princess fairy for good measure. I splattered stars in the sky; robbed from the rich and gave to the poor; and waited in my tower for prince-charming to come with true-love's first kiss. The plans for my life were carelessly and passionately concocted under the limbs of the mighty magnolia tree in my grandparents' back yard. This is where I learned to dream. I was going to be a board game inventor, newspaper editor, voice animator, professional whistler, fashion designer, billionaire-millionaire. And I was going to perform on stages.

I learned to sing in the branches of that magnolia tree. I was fearless and my audience free. The magnolia tree was my Radio City Music Hall, and I was Pavarotti! The magnolia tree was the Olympic floor of life and I vaulted, danced, tumbled, and dreamed my way across the springy floor with childhood bliss and ignorance. The famous gymnastics coach, Bela Karoli, would cheer me on from the upper limbs like he were cheering on Mary Lou Retton. Olympic Gold Medals were at my fingertips. The magnolia tree screamed of my greatness! The branches held within them every possibility in the world. I was destined for greatness!

I dreamed up my whole life under that tree. And the adults in my family gave me permission to do so; encouraged it even.

Did I want to be a firefighter? An astronaut? A prima ballerina? Or the President of the United States? What college would I go to? What great things would I achieve? What type of world-changing person might I become? How many babies would I have? What was my dream car? And would my husband be a lawyer or doctor or perhaps something nobler like a teacher or preacher? Every woman got married, of course.

In this modern American age of privilege and opportunity, every child seems primed to cure cancer or star on Broadway. At the very least, each child deserves a spot on American Idol or their own reality TV series. I think that's why my grandmother made sure my sisters and I watched volumes of the old, black and white Shirley Temple films. "You could do that, Jennifer. You could sing like that little girl." It was the earliest message I received in my tiny corner of the world: You can become anything you want. And you should *want* to become someone amazing. It was our inherent right as American children. Overachieving, exorbitantly paid, famous versions of whoever we wanted to become. Plans that succeeded if we worked hard enough and fame that exploded if we dreamed big enough. The sky was the limit!

A movie reel of heroes, princesses, fairytales, famous athletes, happy endings, and famous people living lifestyles that less than one percent of the world will ever enjoy, splay their way through my earliest memories. *The world is yours for the taking!*

Blurring fantasy with reality as if they are interchangeable, everyday possibilities is our society's blessed curse. Self-made heroes. World-changers. People on a mission, with a plan, in a country where everything is possible if you just *try* hard enough, *work* hard enough, and *plan* far enough in advance.

Do you have goals? Achieve them! Is something standing in your way? Nothing is impossible—just do it!

Under this bold optimism we are sent out to prepare for our future.

Down the road, as a teenager and young adult raised in the evangelical church, *it was expected* that I add in the duty of deciphering 'God's will' and 'God's plan' and the weighty 'purpose' for my existence. Not only was I trying to achieve fairytale love, success, and happiness, but I was doing so with the pressure and confusion of trying to please an all-powerful, invisible God by deciphering His omnipotent will for my life. No. Pressure.

It's a divine miracle that any of us makes it past the first grade, much less our early twenties.

From the moment we enter the world, we are bombarded with equal parts make-believe and future planning. We are taught to dream big and achieve those dreams with a smile on our face and work ethic oozing out of our back pockets. And I am all for optimistic dreaming and the occasional fantasy, I really am. But shouldn't somebody, *somewhere* give a wee heads up about reality?

You know the *this is NOT how I planned it* moments of life.

As privileged children we daydream. We fantasize. We read stories. We perform at Radio City Music Hall—the people at the edge of their seats in awe—we *crescendo*; here comes our big moment where we will bring the world to tears of joy with our giftedness and our beauty and our...

"Dangit, ELLIE! You can't let Jennifer climb the magnolia tree. It's dangerous. She could hurt the TREE!"

Reality interrupts.

Reality trumps dreams.

Reality sneaks in and mocks you. You are no princess. There is no castle. And that tree? It is not a stage; a springboard of all that I will become. It is just a magnolia tree in the back of my grandparents' house, off a gravel road, across from a pond, in a tiny town called Ellisville, right smack dab in the middle of Mississippi.

I'm just a little girl who might hurt the magnolia tree.

Life is complicated. I learned this much when I was six years old.

With the waxy leaves and citrus smell of the mighty magnolia, you rule everything and everyone. You are the master of your own fate. You make plans that don't break and dream dreams that don't crumble. You see the world as it could be, as it *should* be. And every adult cheers you on, hoping you will be more and do more than he or she ever could. *Carpe* freaking *Diem*.

But here? In the real world? A decade or two later, you come face to face with reality. You are not living in a magnolia tree and you are no more a pirate than those weird British fellas that sing pirate songs on TV.

Bills. Babies. Boyfriends. Bosses. Beliefs. Life is not as simple as choosing whether to be an astronaut or the President or a rock star.

It is not black and white and glossy and perfect, the way the seven-year-old mind dreams it to be. Turns out, life is unpredictable. And more times than not, it does not make any sense at all. There are more questions than answers, more in-between spaces, than successfully arrived at finish lines. And it's all quite complicated. The depth of the human soul is complicated. The depth of human experience is complicated. God is complicated. Families are complicated. Friends are complicated. The church is complicated. Lovers are complicated. *Dreaming is complicated.* Living in the tension of big dreams and reality is complicated. It's all cotton candy and nuclear science thrown together in one big pot.

It's never as easy as it was underneath that tree. The big dreams and happy endings that teachers and parents and Disney movies prime you for, those types of endings should be talked about in awe, with hushed voices. Big dreams with happy endings are rare treasures, not inherent rights.

And yet, it's not as simple as making a choice to be a realist or a dreamer. *To dream or not to dream* is not the question. A decision that simplistic means cutting off the head or the heart. But God gave us both head and heart, so what now?

I have decided to let them both exist. Bumping into each other, fighting for space, clashing over the rights to the way I will live my life. Let the head and the heart co-exist, though it makes little sense. Don't forsake dreams for reality. Don't forsake reality for dreams.

There is a complexity in our existence as humans that allow us to embrace both. Without dreams and plans, without vision, the people perish. But don't make those dreams and plans and hold on too tightly, because when reality bites, it bites hard.

This is where I confess: I have no real answers, just a mantra. I will choose to be a dreamer in the face of reality because that is the only way I have found to be fully human. To watch the dreams go up in flames and keep breathing, and dreaming, and trusting that I will become something new all over again. That is where the becoming of all things new is born; in the in-between places.

2 | A BEGINNER'S DREAM

◆

I have two sisters. Melissa is exactly ten and a half months younger than me. Spare yourself the math and *do not* think about how that happened. Every year Melissa and I are the same age from October 6th until my birthday on November 17th. Irish twins.

My other sister, Sarah, is five years younger than me. She was the best little sister ever. She wanted to be friends with Melissa and me so badly that she would let us use her for *all* our childhood experiments. I think this type of loyalty goes a long way in a family.

Every year around Easter, we crucified Sarah.

We wrapped her up in bed linens and tacked her to the wall with thumbtacks. She was a little thing, but the thumbtacks eventually gave way. So when that no longer worked, we ensconced her with couch cushions and pillows, and sometimes got away with tying her hands to a link of sweaters and then bound her to the bedroom door handle. *She was completely okay with this.* Then came the teasing of her hair and the lipstick that doubled as blood on her hands and feet. We might have been slightly confused by the Madonna video, but whatever. My little sister Sarah was an epic Jesus; always so stoic and sad looking. She never fought back. I think that's because she knew Melissa would beat her up.

After Sarah was properly in place for the crucifixion, I popped my Michael W. Smith i2(EYE) cassette tape into the player and fast-forwarded to song number two, *Secret Ambition*.

While Michael sang about nobody knowing that Jesus came to give his life away, Melissa bounced back and forth from being a Roman soldier who had to stab Jesus, to the grieving Mother Mary, and sometimes an angel. She made that angel part up herself. She always thought there should be an angel included in the crucifixion. When she was a Roman soldier she would wear a belt around her head, I thought this was an ingenious use of household supplies. While she was a crying Mother Mary, she put a bath towel over her head. And for the angel role, she would switch to real fairy wings we had left over from a Halloween costume. All the while, Sarah thrashed about in sorrow and played an award-winning Jesus.

And me? I was Michael W. Smith, of course.

Because somebody had to look good, hold the microphone and belt out the passion of the Christ child while baby sister was being crucified.

After our performance was perfect, we did what all normal kids do (because so far, we are *really* tracking with normal kids); we invited our parents and whoever else happened to be in our home that day to the performance. We charged money at the bedroom door and introduced ourselves. Then my parents videotaped and cheered us on as we crucified our little sister.

Completely. Normal. Upbringing.

Sometimes people ask me when I first started singing, or how I knew I wanted to be a musician, as if you can name when you started existing. I tell them I have always sung. I have always created. I have always been a Jenny. It wasn't a career choice or a strategy. It was, as my mom says, present at birth when I ate ferociously at her breast and created melodramas between my dolls and wept through Sesame Street. Perhaps the best answer to the question *when* or *how* lies in the small moments that I decided to stop fighting myself. Fighting who I was. The *when* and *how* happened after I surrendered to the *Who*. I had to surrender to *who* I was before I could fully step into the *when* or *how* of what I would become. I spent a lot of years listening to the whispers in my head that told me I was talking too much or in the spotlight too often. I spent too many years fighting myself, telling myself to be quiet, to be normal. My road to becoming started when I finally told the whispers to shut up. My road to becoming started when I wasn't afraid of my own voice anymore.

I got my first microphone in the fifth grade. On Christmas morning my sisters woke up with board games, a tea set, new clothes, dolls, and other toys that make little girls happy. I only know they got those gifts because I have since studied the pictures. That morning I was oblivious to their gifts and their presence because that morning I got my first karaoke machine. Complete with a microphone, a double cassette tape deck, and three songs on an accompaniment track. *Straight Up* by Paula Abdul, *Crazy* by Patsy Cline, and something else long forgotten. I sang for days, for months, for years.

That same year our school's choir teacher, Mrs. Theiboux, taught us the song *Thank You for the Music*, and I nearly cried every time we got to the chorus. "Thank you for the music! Your gift of friendship rare!" I can still sing that song, word for word, note for note. Fighting back tears in fifth grade choir class because the song so captured my tender heart makes perfect sense to me now. But back then I was sure there was something slightly abnormal going on inside of me. Every day in my public school choir class my heart soared. (And no, it wasn't because I had to be in the tenor section. A real source of middle school insecurity.) We sang Michael W. Smith's *Go West Young Man*, *Get Along Little Doggies*, *The Wabash Cannonball*, *Buh-Bu-Bubblegum*, and Whitney Houston songs. My love for music was solidified. I was head over heels.

During those years, I sang into hairbrushes, paper towel rolls, at the top of my lungs in my garage and sometimes into real microphones. In the sixth grade, I dressed up as Princess Jasmine for the Daniel Intermediate School talent show and sang *A Whole New World* alongside the cutest boy in the entire school. My life was complete.

In the seventh grade, Mrs. McFerrin, the eccentric theater teacher who welcomed you into junior high like you were her long-lost Broadway star, encouraged me to sing loud and proud *and* with animation! I still remember her waddling around the front of the class with her blazing red hair, funky outfits, revered *vibrato*, and intense eyes. In theater class we did songs from the musicals *Newsies* and *Annie*. In eighth grade, we did a full-blown production of *The Wizard of Oz*. I wasn't Dorothy. In fact, I can hardly remember if I was anyone important at all. When I try to recall those seasons, I remember very few specific details about my daily life, but I remember the songs that marked those days.

Music became my everything. Not because of the fame and fortune; it was rare that I actually knew who performed a song. Not because of the history behind it or the mechanics of it; from an early age I disdained learning how to read music and faked my way through sight-reading in every music class I ever took. I still don't know how to read music. Not because I was a song junkie, diving into an artist's catalogue and trying to understand their story and reasons for writing; I didn't care about any of that stuff.

No, music became my everything for the most guttural of reasons. It spoke my language. Finally, someone spoke my language. It was brutal and beautiful all at once. *Brutiful*, as my secret best friend, Glennon Melton, says. Deep and devastating, real and raw, life giving and love-inducing, music gave words to everything that was exploding inside of me.

In high school, I would leave concerts with the friends in my church youth group and I would make sure I sat in the very back row of the van because I knew I would cry. Ugly girl cry. Every show left me a weepy mess. It was as if I had just discovered myself, the beauty of the world and love all over again. We had been at the same show, but I walked away from the experience different than the rest of the group. I wasn't just moved; I was tormented. Something ached within me.

I knew I was supposed to be on stage. Not for the fame and fortune of it. Not for any reason except the most unrefined, obvious one. I was born speaking the language of music. Looking back, I think I left shows with tears running down my face because I realized I was not alone. Artists were living, breathing proof that other people spoke the same language as me. Years later, on my first trip to Nashville to meet with record labels about signing a recording contract, one music executive asked me how I knew I was made for this.

Should I tell him that I left concerts a weepy mess and spent most of the fifth grade begging Jesus to give me *vibrato*? Or that I spent eighth grade pleading for the angelic voice of a soprano, reminding Jesus that being a girl *and* being a tenor was social suicide. Should I tell the Nashville music guy that? There was no litmus test for knowing whether I was normal or insane, or if all artists cried after they went to concerts and prayed such trivial prayers.

I told him the truth. That my ending up in his office was just a blip on the timeline that unfolded over years of singing in my bathroom, garage, church choirs, school choirs and in my closet. I told him about my recurring experiences after concerts and how music was birth, death, life, and everything that lived inside of me exploding in one singular experience. Music was a secret code shared between people living, breathing, and seeing the world with different eyes. Knowing the language existed, knowing it was mine, and yet not quite belonging was torture.

My soul was laid bare in that office with walls covered by platinum albums and pictures of fellow code-talkers. I held my breath and waited for him to call security or politely escort me back to the nice lady who buzzed me into the building. To tell me that I didn't quite fit the rock star bill and that I might be better suited as an elementary choir teacher. Should I tell him I don't really like kids and couldn't read music? I waited for his judgment to fall.

Finally, he looked at me knowingly and smiled. "Every artist I have ever signed to this record label has shared the same sentiment. The true artist feels tormented by the music, by the innate desire to be on that stage. You said exactly what they have said too."

My fears melted. I wasn't crazy.

Something inside me felt fully known and understood. I was not an island. *I was on an island.* An island that spoke about love and death and everything in between through a pounding heart, strings, melodies, and chords. I was a code-talker and I wasn't alone. Perhaps I was a real artist after all.

3 | BIG JOE THE PIMP

◆

I met my husband, Ryan, the first week of my sophomore year in college.

Six weeks before meeting him I had sworn off men once and for all. My heart had just been unexpectedly broken and I wasn't ready for love—only music. But there he was, in the middle of a college-mixer, introducing himself with those ginormous baby blue eyes. He is always mortified when I tell the world that we were at a college mixer for a traveling show choir, *but we were*. A small *Baptist* show choir that performed 1990s Christian music songs with coordinated handclaps. *Of course there were coordinated handclaps.*

Although I had met Ryan several times, I couldn't remember his name. Now those baby blue eyes, I remembered. But I wasn't interested in his name; I was interested in singing.

He asked me out to dinner and I turned him down three times. I couldn't go to dinner because I was headed home—to do my laundry. Coffee? Nope, I had to study. *Dinner on a different night?* I didn't eat dinner. I mean, I ate dinner, but I was "sick" so I couldn't.

He showed up with a can of chicken soup and a roll of crackers and offered to make dinner for me, the "sick girl."

My roommates giggled in the hallway of our apartment. You can't turn a poor boy down when he shows up with chicken soup and baby blue eyes. That was October of 2000. Fourteen months later, the day after Christmas, he proposed to me on a boat as we passed under the Brooklyn Bridge in New York City. Seven months later, two weeks before I started my senior year of college, we got married.

By the time we said *I do*, Ryan and I decided that we could make music and conquer the world. My dad told friends and family gathered at our wedding that they could buy our band's debut album in the church's lobby. Before final exams my junior year in college we drove from Texas to Nashville and used our student loan money (unbeknownst to our parents) to make our first full-length album. It was terrible music. We borrowed my mom's green minivan to make the twelve-hour drive. We had so many people and so much gear in the van that the trunk door wouldn't shut. We bungee corded it shut. It was all kinds of humble beginnings.

Before I started my senior year of college my life had begun to head down a distinct path. It was a path I could have never dreamed up on my own, but I had always known it. Together, Ryan and I created a dream. As wildly young, naive, broke, and totally in love newlyweds we planned out one heck of a far-fetched future together.

When the college career counselors are talking to you about your career goals, you never think you will forgo a grown-up paycheck in order to spend half your week living in a *van* with four boys and the other half living in the *ghetto* with four boys. But this is what happens when you fall in love with a boy and start a band. After graduating from college, my husband, bandmates and I all moved in together. We lived in the hood, the real live hood.

We were not only broke musicians; we were young and naive as well. But we were fearless—living in an eight hundred square foot duplex, forgoing real jobs, working the 5:00 a.m. Starbucks shifts in order to pay the bills and chase our dreams. It was a constant state of bliss and annoyance with one another during that time. Cramped van rides for small, non-paying shows by day; eight hundred square-foot duplex in the ghetto by night.

From what I could tell, the duplex was a complete fire hazard. The fire department confirmed this after we found one of the electrical outlets smoking. The wiring was a ticking time bomb. But it was a toss-up as to what might get us first: electrical fire or the pimp across the street. We decided early on that there was a good chance we might get shot by the pimp, Big Joe. But he came over and decided to become neighborly with us. He said if we wouldn't call the cops on him and would stay out of his business, he would make sure our stuff was never messed with. And Big Joe the pimp was true to his word. We never called the police, and our cars, with tires and hubcaps fully intact, were always there in the morning.

We had no money, no health insurance, no 401(k) plan (Okay, there still isn't. What the heck is that anyway?), and no newlywed family pet. Which apparently is a thing. You get married. You keep a potted plant alive. And then you try your skills out on a dog. But we didn't have a dog. We had bandmates. And as long as our bedroom was located across the hall from the bandmates' bedrooms, I assured my husband we would never have marital relations again. *Never.* I couldn't bear the thought that three other men within eight hundred feet of me might have any clue that *you know what* was happening. So no money, health insurance, 401(k) or family pet, and definitely no sex.

Adulthood started on a gamble. We would conquer our dreams and write our own happily-ever-after one van ride, bad show, late credit card payment, free low-income clinic visit, and sex-less day after another.

Three years after graduating from college, Ryan and I moved into an apartment of our own. Our bandmates moved into the same apartment complex, one building away. We were growing up. Asserting our independence. We signed a record deal with our dream record label and celebrated by buying ourselves one of those giant cookie cakes from the mall. We had them draw a guitar in purple, puffy frosting. We popped open a bottle of champagne, signed the papers in the small living room of our apartment, and celebrated. We made it. Soon we would be on big tours. Our songs would end up on the radio. We would be living in our own tour bus. Recording albums in the heart of Music City. Doing what we loved and what we felt called to. Addison Road. We were the new band in town. And we were living the dream.

4 EPIPHANIES

◆

I was in the third grade when my parents moved my sisters and me from a small, pleasant town in Mississippi to the low-income, drug-ridden side of Fort Worth, Texas. The culture shock was staggering.

In Mississippi, my mom was a youth minister at the local Baptist church and my dad was a police officer. We lived spitting distance from everyone who shared the same blood as us and spent most weekends with our extended family. My early childhood was whiled away roaming through the woods, playing under magnolia trees, and basking in the love of church ladies with sweet tea accents. Life seemed simple and all figured out.

But one day my dad had an epiphany. Epiphanies, I have learned with age, are the root of all evil because they lead to change. And I *despise* change. My dad, *the police officer*, felt like God was leading him away from the police force and into some type of full-time ministry. Like God was inviting him to change the entire course of his life to serve the church. But first he would need to go to seminary. That is the kind of epiphany that, if heeded, can change the course of a man's life.

When I was eight years old my dad decided to go to seminary. And my mom decided to go with him. They listened to the disarming call to drop their nets, like Peter did in the Bible. Like Paul, Moses, Mary and Joseph, Abraham and Sarah, and a whole list of other normal people throughout history who have been divinely invited to change the entire course of their lives to follow God and *live by faith*. My parents' decision wasn't practical, easy, or safe. Living by faith rarely is. It certainly wasn't too well accepted by a family who assumed we would all grow old within spitting distance of one another. But they did it anyway. Moving away from the only home they had ever known, arriving in a new state with no family, raising three small girls, working part time jobs to put food on the table, and attending seminary. *It was a costly epiphany from God.*

"Being a living mystery," Emmanuel Cardinal Suhard says, "Means to live in such a way that one's life would not make sense if God did not exist."

We were officially a *living mystery* kind of family. We arrived in the foreign country of Texas two weeks before I entered the third grade. Three months later, I turned nine years old.

For the first time ever, my mom let me pick out party favors for the friends coming to my birthday celebration. We had always been conservative with money, and now there was never *ever* money, but here she was letting me pick out the most amazing gifts to give my new friends. I chose Lisa Frank gift bags with Lisa Frank stickers and Lisa Frank coloring books for everyone who would come. With a fancy homemade cake and gift bags lining the table and my cutest outfit on, I sat on the front steps of the house, anxiously waiting for the kids to arrive and the party to start.

After a short time and no arrivals, I went into the house and turned on music because music draws people. And then I went back to the porch and waited for kids to come. After more time passed I grabbed the gift bags and brought them outside to the porch, because gift bags draw people. And I waited. Waited for the kids to come. Any kids. I didn't care which ones.

Somewhere in the midst of the waiting, my optimism got the best of me.

Maybe my grandpa would surprise me! Maybe they were just driving in from Mississippi and waiting around the corner, the whole family here to surprise me! Maybe the girls from church were coming. The whole Sunday school class of nameless nine-year-olds I didn't know yet. Or maybe the kids from my new school. Never mind that they spoke Spanish and I spoke English and we couldn't even communicate. Maybe they were coming.

As the minutes ticked away and no one came, I remember my mom wiping tears off her face. I had moved back inside with my family. She was quietly slipping the party bags off the table while my dad took the few presents they were able to afford, unwrapped them, divided them up, and re-wrapped them to make it look like there was more than there actually was. Like maybe I had a friend who had come and brought me a present. Like maybe someone was coming.

Mom, Dad, Melissa, and baby Sarah sang *Happy Birthday* to me. I blew out the candles and opened my presents. And it was still magical. My mom always finds a way to make magic.

At the last minute, a little girl from down the street knocked on the door. It's funny that so many years later I don't remember her name or anything about her, but I have a vivid memory of her face, giant brown eyes, and long, beautiful hair. She was shy and didn't speak English. When she smiled, I saw myself in the silver reflection of her teeth.

She gave me a Barbie wrapped in construction paper.

It was a used Barbie.

With head lice.

In the back bedroom, my mom called her dad and sobbed.

No friends, a used Barbie, and three little girls who now had head lice. She still gets choked up when she remembers the absolute grief that filled her soul in those weeks to follow. Turns out, following God-sized epiphanies doesn't guarantee instant happiness and it might even cost your own children some pain.

In the early days my dad took a job as a security guard at the local hospital to make ends meet. After that he worked at a halfway house for men coming out of prison. Mom joined the staff at a small church where the pastor did bad things with women and stole money from people. My parents attended classes and studied the Bible. My sisters and I fought head lice and language barriers with the neighbor kids and I spent the entire third grade convinced that I might be kidnapped as I walked home from school. I frequently bemoaned our tragic lot in life. Most nights I felt a strange sense of *I-told-you-so* pride when the police helicopters hovered their spotlights on our street, looking for some assailant in the dark. I assured my parents that my sisters and I would be kidnapped and it would be their fault.

Three years later Mom and Dad graduated from seminary. Mom immediately found the perfect job as a student pastor at a church in Duncanville, Texas; the church that ended up being our home for many years. We moved away from police helicopters and drug busts, and into our suburban future. Mom loved her job and we loved not living in fear.

But my dad's future career remained unclear because he couldn't find a job within the church.

Day after day, month after month, year after year. He worked jobs he hated to put food on the table and doubted whether he ever heard God correctly in the first place. For quite some time, Dad lived in a state of dread, shame, and anger.

My dad put it all on the line. Uprooting his family. Changing the entire course of his little girl's lives. Quitting the only career he had ever known and ever been good at to become an ordained minister. And two years after graduating from seminary he was bagging newspapers for minimum wage in the basement of a printing plant in downtown Dallas. Wagering everything on a costly epiphany from God had seemingly gotten him nowhere.

He fought hard. Applying for more jobs than any human being I had known and never giving into the temptation to give up and go back to where he came from and pretend the epiphany never happened. Yet despite his best efforts and my parents' attempts to shield us from the cold, hard truth of it all, we knew. *This wasn't the dream.* I learned when I was a little girl, from the strongest man I knew, that sometimes dreams crash and burn.

5 | UNRAVELINGS

◆

I was in a popular band that had a number one hit on Christian radio and had sold over 100,000 albums when the plans that I made for my adult life started to unravel on a dirty, cornbread covered floor. It was at a Cracker Barrel restaurant in Flagstaff, Arizona.

I sat on the floor of that Cracker Barrel, unaware of the rest of the world, and let the tears drip off my chin. Among my snot and tears, I spent two hours batting cornbread crumbs and well-worn pegs from the classic triangle game out of my eleven-month-old-baby's mouth. What kind of mother ends up stranded at Cracker Barrel? Letting her kid eat cornbread crumbs off the floor? My baby would need therapy by the time she was seven. That was the only thing I could think about.

Addison Road was four days into the spring tour of 2010, alongside the band Sanctus Real, when we found ourselves somewhere between Albuquerque, New Mexico, and Flagstaff, Arizona, running on fumes.

But the truth is that my husband and I had been running on fumes for much longer than that.

It started a year earlier, March 2009, during my eighth month of pregnancy.

Fifty pounds heavier than normal, I waddled down three flights of stairs at our apartment complex, excited to be leaving on what would be Addison Road's biggest tour ever. Yes, *leaving*. In reality we only sang four songs the entire night, which was a good thing since I had a small alien living inside of me who was making it nearly impossible to breathe. But we could have just been singing one song and I would have been happy. We had spent the better part of our career as an independent band playing small church gigs with horrible sound systems and fifty people in the audience. Arenas with 15,000 people and jumbo-trons felt like a dream come true. A national tour with internationally known artists in sold-out arenas! We felt like we had finally made it and the tour couldn't start fast enough. At eight months pregnant I was headed into twelve concerts, across twelve states, and I was ready to conquer the world.

By the time I reached the bottom of the stairs the morning we were leaving for the tour, my husband Ryan had already made it to the van and was walking back toward the apartment. "Did you forget something, baby?" I asked, giddy with excitement.

He walked right past me. Eyes glazed over.

"Hey, where are you going? Did you forget something?" I asked again, a little more puzzled.

Ryan is type-A. He likes to sleep in beds with sheets that are perfectly folded and tucked into the corners. Once, he bought a contraption that printed off labels so he could properly label our infant daughter's travel toiletries. He is structured. Organized. And annoyingly perfect. He doesn't forget things, so I felt a small degree of panic. I remember the look on his face that day as he walked past me on the stairs. I will always remember it.

"RYAN!" I yelled, trying to get his attention.

For a moment I could tell he couldn't even hear me yell his name. And then he turned around.

"Jen, our van and trailer are gone. Everything. It's all gone. It's not where I parked it. It's not... I'll call the police. You call the guys."

He kept walking up the stairs with an unflinching gaze of focused direction. I stood with my mouth wide open.

When you are pregnant, sometimes you have moments of insanity. I thought this might be one such moment. Maybe I was hallucinating. Maybe I was confused. Maybe I didn't hear him right. He kept walking up the stairs, placing calls, springing into action. And I wandered the parking lot as if perhaps we had simply misplaced our big white van and big white trailer. Because that was the answer I really wanted to hear in that moment. Not that we were robbed.

We left on the *Rock and Worship Road Show* tour the next day in a rented van. No trailer. No instruments. No merchandise to sell, which was the only way to make money on the tour since we weren't being paid much. We had nothing but our suitcases. It was the first time I had experienced the loss of my "stuff." In that moment it's not so much the stuff that has been stolen that shakes you, but the feeling of insecurity in your own home that robs you of your freedom to live without fear.

The following week we were scheduled to be home for forty-eight hours and we were moving. I decided in a *don't-mess-with-the-pregnant-woman* type moment that we would not be raising our daughter in an apartment complex where entire vans and trailers just up and disappear. What kind of apartment complex lets that happen? It was settled.

We would tear down my daughter's perfectly put-together nursery, I would pack up my reading room with the beautiful floor-to-ceiling windows, and we would move in forty-eight hours' time and then hit the road again. This is what all eight-months-pregnant women enjoy doing on their two days off. Moving away from robbers.

My friend Krista met me and took me to her side of town where vans and trailers don't disappear. She shuttled me around the neighborhood with the seriousness of a private investigator. We were on a mission and she was the private eye, detective, bodyguard, and "don't-mess-with-Jenny-she's-pregnant" mama bear that I desperately needed in that moment. She haggled with apartment people for me, using the robbery and my emotional pregnant state as persuasive leverage and got us the lowest rent anyone has paid on *that side of town* in a long time.

In two days' time, we found a perfect neighborhood; our friends and family had completely packed our apartment, carted it down three flights of stairs, and moved us across the city. We left the next morning while other people unpacked us into our new home. Other people deciding where the dishes went. Other people setting up my first-born daughter's nursery. Other people playing house for us.

There was still no sign of the van or the trailer. No sign of the instruments and merchandise and the vehicle that we used to make a living. No sign of getting back what we lost. So we settled into the idea that we would just have to count it a loss, wait for the insurance money to kick in, and move forward. We had no clue lightning would strike more than once. That it would strike twice, three times, maybe four. We had no idea this was the beginning of the end.

Looking back, if I had to pick a moment, well, that would be the one. The moment everything started to fall apart and my plans began to unravel. Annie was born two weeks later. She was the silver lining.

6 | A BAD YEAR

◆

My favorite book growing up was *Alexander and the Terrible, Horrible, No Good, Very Bad Day*.

Alexander has a really bad day. Alexander wakes up late and he misses the bus. His brother gets new shoes, but the store is out of shoes in his size. His siblings get ice cream, but his falls right off the cone. He steps in gum. He swallows toothpaste. He has to go to bed early. And he is convinced that his mom likes his brother better than him. His solution is almost always moving to Australia.

"I think I'll move to AUSTRALIA!" he laments.

And even as a kid, I knew he was on to something. Because some days you just want to stay in bed. Or move to Australia.

I began to think of the first year of my daughter's life as the Terrible, Horrible, No Good, Very Bad Year. It was like a bad day; the kind where you make it halfway through the morning and find yourself cursing your existence and rolling your eyes at all the annoying, happy people around you. But the bad day dragged on and eventually became months, and finally crept into a year. My daughter's first year on planet earth was the hardest year of my life and she, the new crying baby who refused to sleep, was my only reprieve. When your first-born baby is the *easiest* part of your life, there is a serious problem.

Those are the kinds of days, turned weeks, turned months that drive people to their weaknesses. Working out. *TMZ* marathons. Vodka. Self-medicating. Tracking down old flings on Facebook. In my case, Ben and Jerry's ice cream, *Oprah* reruns, and an unwritten sign on my back that perpetually read *Mean Girl*. Okay *and a season of too much vodka*. A year of brokenness led me to becoming the worst possible version of myself.

By September of 2009 we had finally collected all of the insurance money and were able to replace our van, trailer, music equipment, in-struments, and merchandise. But the toll of the financial stress that had accrued in the meantime, continuing to tour, and doing it all with my five-month-old baby in tow was mounting. My primary doctor told me I was the youngest patient she had ever diagnosed with Shingles and asked in a sharp voice if I planned on my life becoming less stress-ful in the near future. I stared at her blankly. That's like asking some-one if they plan on having less cancer in the future. *I sure hope there is less stress, lady.*

Three weeks after the Shingles diagnosis we lost the van and trailer all over again. I wasn't in the van; I just got the phone call. It was late at night and there was heavy rain. They were on a dark country road; there was a curve, then a blind spot, and an oak tree that had fallen squarely in the middle of the street. The guys in the band were okay and that's all I cared about. But the van and trailer- *the brand new van and trailer-* were a total loss. The loss was so unreal it was almost comi-cal. We were living in a perpetual plague of grasshoppers, crickets, frogs, and thefts. We were so Old Testament. We were in a bloody river.

By March of 2010 almost a year had passed since our van and trailer were stolen and our baby was born. Nearly six months since the Shingles appeared and the van and trailer had been totaled in the wreck. And then coming full circle, as if to tie up the year from hell with a pretty bow, there was that one particular week in March 2010 that I will never forget.

On Monday we came back defeated from a weekend of poorly attended shows and found that both of our personal cars had died. For the first time in our adult lives we didn't have the money in the bank to fix them. On Tuesday my baby cousin drove over an improvised explosive device in his armored medical vehicle in Afghanistan and he was fighting for his life. My family was broken as we waited on the jumbled updates. On Wednesday Annie woke up from her afternoon nap with blood running out of her ears and down her neck. She needed emergency surgery. And we needed $3,000 to pay the deductible; I had to call my dad and painfully, shamefully ask for money. On Thursday Annie had surgery. And on Saturday we flew to Albuquerque, New Mexico, to begin the spring tour of 2010.

In retrospect, leaving home after a week like that—a year like that—seems foolish. But in the moment, leaving seemed like the most logical answer. Something had gone really wrong during the first year of Annie's life. We knew that much. We were living in a plague of Old Testament proportions and it felt like we were cursed. Ryan and I convinced ourselves that the way out of our suffering was running away.

To Albuquerque, then Phoenix, Las Vegas, California, and Oregon. Shows were scheduled back to back for two months straight with Sanctus Real. And that was the answer; the cities, people, shows. The anywhere-but-here. As if you can magically dust curses off your hands like sand off your sandals and move to the next town where you are wanted. But running away almost never makes things better. We should have heeded the lesson from Jonah in the Old Testament. His running away earned him a spot in the guts of a whale.

If you are lucky, running prolongs your time a bit. But if you are really having a go at it, the breakdown of your dreams and plans seems to follow you whether you are on a plane, in an RV, or in Australia. You can't outrun life's unraveling no matter how hard you try. Still, we tried. We hit the road. It was March 2010.

7 CORNBREAD CRUMBS

◆

Most insurance companies were avoiding us like the plague, which limited our ability to purchase a vehicle to travel in, so we decided to rent. The RV we rented came from another couple in the music industry who also traveled with their children. They let us rent their home on wheels while they were on Sabbatical from road-life. This was a huge gift. The RV was smallish and older, but brimming with life. By the looks of our luggage and junk food we could have passed for a tribe of eighth grade girls headed to band camp. Five band members, a nanny, a cute baby (who was only four days post-surgery) and a driver. We were a motley, excited crew.

There were enough clothes on board to open a Goodwill store. My type-A man prepared the RV as if it were a submarine that would not emerge from the deep for a year. Kitchen appliances, vacuum cleaner, coat hangers, cups, cleaning supplies. Anything our daughter might possibly need tucked away into her own magical wonderland in the back bedroom. Toys, books, stuffed animals, movies, a pack-and-play, and a fenced-in bed so she and I could safely spend time together as we drove.

The excitement in leaving the past behind and facing a new adventure was teeming up in our home on wheels. Taking pictures, eating junk food, making spring tour predictions, and planning out practical jokes; we felt like teenagers headed to summer camp. The first drive was from Albuquerque to Phoenix. The six of us, plus baby, spent much of the morning in the front lounge talking about the album we had just finished recording and flipping through radio stations to see if anyone was playing our new single yet. It felt like the escape I so desperately hoped it would be. I soaked in every glorious moment.

I suppose that's why I didn't notice that somewhere in the desert between New Mexico and Arizona the RV started feeling a bit warm and driving a bit sluggish. Perhaps the joy of the moment helped us discount the smell of diesel fumes blanketing the inside of our home on wheels. Perhaps that's why none of us seemed to be alarmed, or even notice, when the RV refused to creep past the forty miles per hour it was traveling at. Slow decay is hard to spot and even harder to acknowledge.

We were in the middle of the desert when the heat began to bear down on us. The nearest city was Flagstaff. The last hour of the drive the RV hovered at thirty miles an hour. The nanny vomited the entire time. We were crawling at a torturous pace, on a torturous drive, and had made a torturous career choice. By this point it was undeniable that we were decaying. If at one point we felt like teenagers headed to summer camp, we now felt like full-grown adults waiting in a hospital as someone we loved died. No one spoke.

We knew we had to make it to a city where the RV could be brought back to life, but the conditions were bleak. With each breath of exhaust fumes in, I let out a breath of defeat. I was suffocating. Weariness, anger, and hopelessness coursed through my lungs. *Really, Lord?* My anger was palpable. It was one thing to remain faithful to a calling when my life was the only one on the line. But now Annie's was too. I had never known such guilt.

Our eleven-month-old, beautiful little girl, who never asked to be put on airplanes and deserved better than a life lived in the back of an RV, was breathing in the exhaust fumes too. That little girl with the big blue eyes and a smile that changed every orbit she entered was coughing and sweaty. Only seven days post-surgery. The smoke. The fumes. The headaches. The blurry eyes. Those were hers too. How could I be doing this to her? What kind of mom allows this to happen to her child?

I was suffocating on the fumes. But what was really choking the air out of my soul was the overwhelming guilt I felt for dragging my daughter into my own cursed existence. In the heat of that muggy, broken RV I began to fight the final blows of a battle I knew I was going to lose.

We made it to Flagstaff before we finally broke down on the side of the highway, with seven sweaty adults, a baby, and a broken RV.

I did what any mom would have done if she were stranded on the side of the highway.

I Googled local churches and started calling until I got someone on the line.

Through tears and absolute authority I said, "Hi. My name is Jenny. I'm a Christian band. I mean, I'm *in* a Christian band. I mean I AM A CHRISTIAN and my baby and I are stranded on the side of *your* highway. And since we are both Christians YOU ARE MORALLY OBLIGATED to come pick us up!"

Two churches put me on hold. Indefinitely. But one sweet lady, unafraid of my completely psychotic story and voice said, "Huuunny, my husband drives a white pickup. He'll be over there to fetch you in just a bit."

And he came. The man morally obligated to pick up the Christians on the side of the highway came! He took us girls to the local Cracker Barrel, and he carted the boys off to the airport so they could get rental cars. The manager at Cracker Barrel, God love him, let me set up shop in part of the restaurant that wasn't being used. The employees were all angels to the slightly crazy woman and her cute baby.

And my eleven-month-old baby crawled around on the floor while I constantly swatted pieces of cornbread crumbs out of her hands and wiped tears and snot off my own chin. Based on all those pretty little books at Barnes and Noble, this was *not* what to expect for my baby's first year. This was not what it was supposed to look like when I listened to a holy voice that said, *Come; follow me.* This was not what I imagined when I decided to chase my dream of writing music that would change the world. This was not what other successful artists looked like. *None* of it was going the way it was supposed to go.

Tear by tear, cornbread crumb after cornbread crumb, a quiet despair overcame me. *This wasn't the dream.* Good thing I learned when I was a little girl, from the strongest man I knew, that *sometimes* dreams crash and burn. Because I was crashing and about to burn—literally.

8 | THE END OF THE ROAD

◆

My husband made the call to leave the RV at a repair shop in Flagstaff and rent cars in order to make it to the show that night in Phoenix. We would pack what we needed for the evening; spend the night in Phoenix after the concert and the RV would meet us the next morning, ready to drive us to Las Vegas for the next night's show in Sin City.

I packed lightly. Everything fit into Annie's diaper bag. I was convinced, after all, that the RV would be fixed sooner than we thought. I might even be able to get back to Annie's room in the RV before we went to bed that night. It was just going to be an easy fix and our home on wheels would be a few short hours behind us. Based on our track record I should have assumed the worst, but my survival instincts kicked in. I believed the best because it was all I had left.

The RV was in fact, not ready to meet us in Phoenix that night *or* the next morning and we had to make a decision. Go back to where we broke down, in Flagstaff, Arizona, and wait for our RV to get repaired or keep the rental cars and head on to the next show in Las Vegas, Nevada. With a few guitars, duffle bags, and the clothes on our backs, we kept the rental cars and drove to Las Vegas, mostly empty-handed.

We didn't have *any* of our merchandise, because it didn't fit in the rental cars. All three thousand t-shirts, CDs and other merchandise trinkets you sell in order to pay the bills while you're out touring, was in the trailer, attached to the RV. Computers, credit card machines, clothes, diapers, suitcases, underwear, baby toys, blankets, and all the special embroidered gifts that first babies get was in the RV... all of it. We weren't prepared to last more than a short night and morning away from our home on wheels. But we didn't want to miss the sold-out show in Las Vegas either. So we arrived at the venue with the outfits on from the night before and borrowed musical gear from our tourmates. I had two diapers left and was hopeful Annie would not have the classic, mustard blowout she was notorious for.

Sometime that night, during dinner, Ryan got a call. He looked confused. He left the room. He came back. Ash white. Eyes wide with adrenaline and a twisted smirk on his face. He was smiling so he wouldn't crack and break.

The RV had blown up.

There was a single explosion underneath the bed that Annie and I spent our time on. A fireball shot fifty feet into the sky. There were pictures. Our driver, Brandon, was sending video clips. He was somewhere in the desert outside of Las Vegas. Initially, he blacked out because the smoke was so heavy. The highway was shut down; police, firefighters, and paramedics were all on the scene. Everything was in flames. Less than five minutes and it all burned to the ground. It was all gone.

We gathered around Ryan's phone to watch our world go up in flames with our driver's words coming over the phone, hanging in mid-air. Gone. Explosion. Nothing left. What to do with the remains? My head was spinning. The world seemed to disappear; the voices grew blurry.

We were told it took state troopers six hours and specialized equipment to remove the RV's metal frame from the highway because it melted right into the asphalt.

I was told it took specialized equipment to keep me breathing.

I had a complete breakdown.

Ryan and I lost everything that night. Besides the furniture and dishes back home, everything we owned was on that RV. Everything we owned had blown up. Five minutes and it all stopped existing. And after the year from hell, this was too much for me to bear.

I found a small, empty children's nursery in the back of the church where the concert was being held. And I fell apart. I remember every single detail. The cracker crumbs on the floor, the taste of my tears, the feeling of nausea that overcame me, the disorientation, the ticking of the clock, the laughing voices of teenagers passing in the hall as if nothing had happened. As if life were easy and fair. I distinctly remember feeling a surge of rage.

Can't they be quiet? Just shut up and stop being stupid teenagers... my mind and heart raged. Then I folded into a ball as uncontrollable sobs heaved out of my body.

The hardest part of suffering is that the rest of the world keeps going like nothing has happened.

Years ago I sat next to my husband's grandmother in the hospital as she lay dying. My mother-in-law ran her fingers through Nanny's hair and said, "It's okay, Mama. Go home and be with Jesus. Go be with Daddy. Go home, Mama. It's okay to go now." We sang an old hymn to her, *I Go to the Garden Alone.* Tears fell; the silence wringing our souls out. Her breathing became more labored; each breath shorter than the one before. Each pause between breaths drawing us all closer to heaven. Each pause excruciating as Nanny fought hard to stop fighting.

And the nurses were talking way too loudly in the hallway. A little kid was running down the corridor screaming. Someone was honking their horn outside. And there were construction workers with cranes and equipment, banging and banging and banging their tools on the street below.

And I just wanted to yell at all of them, *Stop! Be quiet! Our world is breaking in here. We are walking Nanny to heaven. She is going to the freaking garden alone; please just stop.*

As I wept on the floor of that nursery in Las Vegas, wrestling with the final blow of the year that seemed to rob me of everything, my weary soul wanted the whole world to just stop. Everything in my soul wanted to beg the world around me for what it could not possibly give.

Just give me a minute to grieve—to wrap my mind around this—please just stop with me.

But the world can't stop for every heartbreak.

If it did, it would never start again. So it keeps going. Little babies are born and people leave this life and pass on to the next with each tick of the clock. Diseases are diagnosed, art is created, marriages fall apart, community happens, people give up, orphans are rescued, businesses fail, cures are discovered, and earthquakes shake the foundation of the very thing we have come to rely on as constant.

And those who still have solid ground underneath them? They must keep going.

The world doesn't stop for life or death or breakdowns or earthquakes, and it certainly doesn't stop for fires.

The loneliness I experienced when my life went up in flames is hard to explain. When the world keeps going in spite of your suffering, you begin to realize that true grief is observed alone. What a harsh insult to injury. I know now there are some journeys you have to walk alone, no matter how many people love you; no matter how many friends you have; no matter what kind of community you surround yourself with.

The hardest part of my world crumbling was realizing that nobody else's was. At least not in the same way mine was.

Not even my husband's, who lost the same exact belongings as me. A grief, truly observed, happens deep within the confines of your own soul. And if no two souls are the same, it stands to reason, no season of grief is the same either. Grief is unique like freckles, isolating like puberty sprouting deep in your bones, private like discovering the curves of your own body.

And it was there, in that most private, desolate, lonely place, where no one else could truly stop, could truly make their way to the depths of my despair with me, that I remember with certain, haunting clarity

her voice

and his eyes.

9 | ANTS AND OTHER HOLY THOUGHTS

◆

I took my first breath in between the rock, painted deserts, and rugged mountains of New Mexico. It was November 17, 1980, at Saint Joseph's Hospital in Albuquerque. If ever a place has owned me, New Mexico has—I can't get enough of it.

Orange and pink sunsets burn golden edges on the horizon. They are the canvases on which God proclaims most deeply to me that He is holy and kind. Majesty is laid bare in every corner of the state; it doesn't take much effort to see why they call it the *Land of Enchantment*. Enchantment is everywhere. In unassuming cliff dwellings and pine trees needling through the clouds, white sand as far as the eye can see and winding mountain roads. Rainstorms blow in, and from a distance it looks like all of heaven has opened up to pour out dancing streams of water onto thirsty ground. I'm convinced it's one of the most sacred places in the world, and that is why I return to New Mexico year after year.

For years I have wanted to hike a mountain outside of Santa Fe called Baldy. I'm not a hiker and I'm not in the kind of physical shape that I want to be in. I don't own good hiking boots or even a decent water bottle. I hate bugs, dirt, and all forms of discomfort. I get dizzy at high altitudes and I have an absolutely terrible propensity to quit anything I am doing if I get even the slightest stomach cramp. I guess you could say I'm *not* hiking material.

Still, I felt like I should hike this mountain that lies on the outer edge of a camp that I have been going to my whole life. Everyone always talks about hiking Baldy and how beautiful it is at the top. It's sort of a badge of honor to hike the trail; a way of identifying yourself as a true alumnus of the camp. So with fear and trepidation, I decided to take the plunge and earn the merit badge.

I went on the hike with two goals in mind: staying alive and walking away with a good story.

Preferably some deep revelation about God and hard work and earning merit badges and being on the mountaintops of life.

This particular summer, my enthusiastic, athletic, gorgeous friend Chelsie was at camp with me and agreed to make the hike. With water bottles and little else in tow, we set off one morning on the seven-mile trek. My eyes were wide open. Looking for the story. *Or bugs.* Waiting for a moment of deep truth to hit me. *Or for a leg cramp to give me an excuse to quit.* Past trees that shot up hundreds of feet in the air, critter holes, boulders, and infinity edges that gave you a view of the beautiful forever, we trudged. Sometimes talking. Sometimes just trying to breathe.

We were surrounded by hundreds of trees. Thin air and mountains on every side of us. When we finally stopped in a clearing to catch our breath, we couldn't see the camp anymore. At an earlier point we saw it, seemingly thousands of miles behind us looking like a tiny dot, but now it was nowhere in sight. Neither was the edge of the mountain or the beautiful New Mexico forever.

We were somewhere deep in between. Tangled up in trees that towered over us on every side, climbing high in front of us and behind us. It was shaded, darker, and there was a chill rushing down the mountain.

Chelsie stood, hands on her hips, looking all around us as if she were studying our exact location, drawing a picture of it in her head. I sat down on a dead tree branch to drink the last of the water and was promptly attacked by red ants the size of beetles. I bemoaned the number of ants in the world, shocked that they were thriving at such high altitudes.

"How many ants do you think there are in this world?" I whined, "I mean, really, do they have to be on mountains too? Ugh! I hate ants." I brushed the ants off and picked up sticks so that I could attack them.

Chelsie, eyes still studying the trees above us, spoke as if she had not heard a word I said, "You know Jen, even if we were to get lost up here, not visible to any helicopter or search team, just lost somewhere like a speck in the midst of a million trees, we would not be lost to God. God would know exactly where we are. That's amazing. He could find us. You know, He could find us out here. He can pinpoint us right now. He is the only one who knows. "

I looked at her, annoyed.

I have climbed this mountain all morning, hoping for some sort of spiritual revelation like this and all I have walked away with is a deep worry that ants are taking over the world.

While I spent my time reasoning that for every tree on that mountain there were probably a hundred thousand million ants, she was walking around thinking holy thoughts. I am cursing ants and she's realizing that from where we stand, in the midst of a million trees, the human eye cannot see us, but God can still see us. Only God can see us. We didn't have enough water or time to make it to the top of the mountain. So we sat a bit longer in the clearing then started our journey down.

    Exactly one year later, with a new hiking partner in tow, better shoes and in better shape, I found myself attempting to hike to the top of the mountain again. This time I wanted to make it to the top. To the tippy top of the tippy top, seven miles up. We were determined. We started at 7,000 feet and we would end at 11,000 feet. We would end at 11,000 feet. We would end at 11,000 feet. We would end at…

Maybe just 9,000 feet? 9,000 feet would be good enough, wouldn't it? My bandmate, Richard, and I took turns quitting on each other. He wanted to stop and go back down but I charged ahead. I wanted to stop. I whined and complained and cried tears of pathetic failure. "But we are so close. We're like, almost practically there," he would say.

But this was a complete lie. Neither of us knew how much longer we actually had, because neither of us knew where we were. Or when we left. Or how far we had already traveled. We set out on the hike the way a kid sets out to find Santa Claus in the woods behind their backyard, entirely naive and unprepared to hike to the North Pole.

I needed food, water, and sustenance. That morning I skipped the cafeteria breakfast. Thirteen hundred other people had already been through the line. Twenty-six hundred hands digging serving spoons into silver pales of lumpy eggs, mixed with the overpowering smell of chlorine-mopped floors? I would quite honestly rather eat my big toe. So I had a banana and a piece of toast with honey. That was five hours before the hike.

What was I thinking? Mental torture ensued as my feet dragged me toward the top of a mountain I now despised. There weren't enough calories in me for an ant to make it up and down a mountain. How could I have been so dumb? Would my dad find my body or a park ranger? Or would a GRIZZLY BEAR EAT MY DEAD BODY FIRST?

Richard and I both tried quitting on each other one more time. We quit on the mountain, on life, on the people joyfully passing us with their fancy REI water bottles, compasses, and hiking sticks. We hated them, as a matter of fact.

My ears were burning. Deep inside they just hurt. It was the wind and the altitude and the cold air and the deep out-of-shape breathing that got my ears all burning and tingling inside. The pain went down the side of my neck and I felt it at the base of my head. My hair hurt and my fingernails felt brittle, like the wind was blowing through them. Mostly though, it hurt to swallow.

Not like a sore throat, but a dry throat. My mouth was dry. My throat was dry. As if deep crevasses had broken into the lining of my vocal chords, cracked wide by the desert sun, split open into parched tunnels. My spit was gone, and even trying to get spit from somewhere else hurt.

I was so frustrated at myself. Why didn't I save my spit? I knew better than that. I *knew* to save my spit. If I learned anything in my childhood it was this: a smart kid saves their spit.

On long car rides, Dad would always say, "We're not stopping for another hour, so if you're thirsty you better start saving that spit!" On camping trips, we would hear the same thing. "We're going to the top and once you run out of water in your bottle don't ask to drink from your sister's bottle. You better just save your spit." Save your spit to make snowmen. Save your spit to drink later on in the car. Save your spit to clean your face off (that one I learned from my grandpa). The whole world had a thing about spit saving.

Why didn't I listen to the man? I didn't even know how much longer I had. There were no mile markers. No trail signs. Just dense forest and pathways that led further and further up. I would have killed for spit.

The trees were hanging over us. My muscles burned. My stomach cramped. My feet felt like lead. And it wasn't fun anymore. No rush. No mountain high. No spiritual revelations. No merit badges for sportsmanship or good work ethic or pure thoughts. My thoughts were sooo not pure. Richard and I weren't talking anymore, just huffing and puffing. Why did I insist on doing this?

And that's when I heard His voice.

Like the trees were whispering, His Spirit descended on me, taking up my insides. Like all of Narnia was coming out from under the spell of ice and breathing itself on me and in me. I heard an overwhelming voice on that mountain speak a profound truth into me.

It was overwhelmingly quiet and simple.

"I thirst."

That was it. I thirst.

And it all started to make sense to me. Like a movie fast-forwarded to the end and then re-wound and re-played. I saw the pieces of my faith come together, the story of Jesus playing out in front of my eyes.

The insult. The alcohol offered to a thirsty, dying man. The vinegar. The oil. The pain of being thirsty. The burning ears. The throat. Even the tips of His hair hurting. Gasping.

And all of a sudden, on that mountain, I realized the cost of grace.

In the most unlikely moment, when I had given up on any spiritual revelations and conceded to death-by-grizzly-bear, I finally understood that I was not alone in my suffering, because Jesus had been thirsty too.

Lots of people have been thirsty. Have gone thirsty. Have died thirsty. But their thirst does not bring me strength, only guilt.

His thirst though? The Son of God's thirst digs down deep into me and saves me. His grace came with a price; He thirsted. And for the first time in my life, I understood the physical pain of being thirsty. And I felt a deep sadness.

I wish Jesus never had to feel thirsty.

At the tippy top of the tippy top of the mountain, the only mountain I have ever used my own legs to climb, I was surrounded by ants. And wind, other mountains, a million trees, the fear of bears, the dread of descent, and the piercing sound of utter silence. And I felt the kind of alone that feels independent at first. Then it just feels kind of lonely. Kind of scary. I was ready to go home and be done.

So this is what it feels like to be thirsty, I thought. Grace burned the back of my throat. To know what it feels like to be that kind of thirsty and that kind of lonely made Jesus seem a little more near, a little more real than He had ever seemed. I thought of my friend Chelsie and how she only had to walk a short while to realize the vastness of where we were and the way it could make us feel lost. She knew what it felt like to be lost, but she wasn't afraid because she knew what I didn't. Not only could God see us in our lostness, He could empathize.

She understood. We would be thirsty and might get lost. And that was okay, because Jesus was thirsty too. And that meant He knew how to find us.

ᔫ

I felt thirsty on the floor of that nursery in Las Vegas.

First, I called my dad.

"Dad," I sobbed, "You gotta come get me. I'm in Vegas with no clothes."

That is a call that *every* father dreams of getting from his little girl. It went over real well.

Then I called my dear friend and pastor, Jackie Roese, and unleashed a torrent of emotion.

She responded to me firmly, with her tender, authoritative New York accent. She held my hands over the phone.

"Listen to me. You gotta pull it together. You can do this. You lock eyes with Him, Jenny. No one else. No one else has you right now. Just Him, Jenny. It's just you and Jesus. You lock in with everything you have. Picture Him standing in front of you. Now look into His eyes. Nowhere else. Lock in. You can do this. Don't look to the left or the right or up or down; you look Jesus in the eyes, Jenny. Nowhere else."

It was her voice and His eyes.

I had never felt so lonely in my life. My throat burned. I felt dizzy. My legs were shaky. I felt sick to my stomach on the floor of that room. I called Jackie to tell her, through unintelligible sobs, that there was an explosion and we were okay, but our RV and everything we owned was gone. Burned up in a fire that had the entire highway shut down. To tell her that, and also that I was done. With ministry. With being faithful. With being sweet. With everything. I was done. And I needed to come home and cuss and drink and scream and quit and cry. There were so many tears I needed to cry. Can someone just come get me? I *actually* asked her that.

Come scoop me off the floor, wrap me up in a blanket, hold me in their arms, put me in a bed somewhere, and nurse me back to life.

And the opening band went on stage. And the ladies in the green room cleaned up scraps from dinner. And my daughter played with our nanny. And my husband made calls to insurance companies and police officers. And the teenagers in the hallway laughed and ran around while my spirit crumbled and gave up in that little room 2,000 miles away from home.

I had never been so thirsty.

I knew in that moment a complete brokenness that you can only experience by yourself. I was at the very end of my own capacity to survive. This was what it meant to be thirsty. It meant to be alone in the most severe of ways. My tears finally dried up. And I sat in silent on the phone. There was nothing left. But she was still there on the line. Still holding me together through the phone.

And that's why I remember her voice and His eyes.

"Jenny," Jackie said with a tenderness I can still feel, "This is an awesome place to be. An awesome place to be. This is the best night of your life. The *best* night."

Her voice hung in the air. I was too weak to protest.

"This is the best night of your life because Jenny, *you are about to see God be God.*"

And with eight words, my life was on the path to being reborn.

I didn't know it then. But she did. Because every good pastor knows that death leads to life.

10 | THE END

◆

In December 2010, after the longest, most successful tour Addison Road had ever been a part of, my husband quit the band. We were exhausted and we were financially ruined from the events of the past two years. We were on the brink of bankruptcy as a band and well past that as a couple. Our credit was ruined, we were in debt to everyone who had been keeping us afloat during all the losses, and no insurance company would touch us with a ten-foot pole. The longer Addison Road existed, the more we lost.

I was a thirty-year-old-woman, with a husband, daughter, and songs on the radio. Yet I was driving my barely drivable car from high school, circa 1999, living in a tiny apartment and still asking my dad to help pay the bills. Only now, I was asking through shame and tears and exhaustion.

Ryan and I prayed about the decision for months, but it was clear, he had to quit and get a job. We would figure the rest out as we went. But that one part was non-negotiable. Our community stood by us and gave us courage. Our friend Gregg, who has lived a little more life than us, took Ryan out for coffee. He told Ryan that what he was doing would ultimately be good, but initially it would feel like a death. A loss so heavy and deep that he would be tempted to turn around and run back the other way. The way he came from and knew. Gregg said he would be there for Ryan when that temptation to turn around and go back was too strong. And he was. He has been there for us every step of the way.

The decision was made. We knew it deep down in our souls, but acting on it was almost impossible. First we disguised it as a break, and said we needed two months off the road. We put off the inevitable for weeks. We avoided the reality of it all. We learned that the hardest part is doing what you already know you need to do. And each day we fought hard to quit fighting it. It's nearly impossible to admit when you are staring it in the eyes, but sometimes a death is the best possible thing that can happen.

I'm still in awe of how my husband let go with grace. How he quit the fight and let something precious to him die.

Ryan felt a deep sense of peace about moving forward. It was the first time I had seen peace on his face in years. Relief. The relief that comes when someone you love finally gets to quit fighting the disease and go be with Jesus. The fight was suffocating every part of us. And as Ryan surrendered to quitting and took his last breath with the band, peace washed over us. It felt so good not to fight. It felt free.

We decided that I would stay in the band, he would find a desk job to help stabilize our financial situation, and we would just take it one day at a time and figure out a new normal.

Our bandmates gathered in our living room one morning as Ryan told them that after eleven years he needed to move on. As he spoke, I held my breath. What would the other guys say? What would the future of being in a band without my husband look like? What comes next for Addison Road?

What came next was mass mutiny.

They all quit. They all felt released. They all had peace wash over their faces like I hadn't seen in years. And before the morning was over, my husband and bandmates of eleven years were deciding who got to quit the band *first* over a game of Farkel. They laughed and joked like little boys who were free. I never imagined the end would be so beautiful.

Quitting *en masse* to start over from scratch turned out to be one of God's most kind blessings. Watching the guys I loved love each other well as we worked on resumes, ending the band with love and integrity, honoring our final contracts, and not being tempted to avoid the unknown future by clinging to the past was a rare gift. The most beautiful break-up one can imagine. And we stepped into a blank page, side-by-side, unwilling to let one another turn back around to the life we were leaving behind, simply because we did not yet know exactly what the future might hold.

The guys seemed to have a peace about moving forward and an idea of where they were headed. In fact, four short months later, when the rest of the world still thought Addison Road was a band, they were full-time employees holding down forty-plus-hour-a-week jobs. They had the kind of peace that sent them down a new path with confidence. But I had none. My moving forward was only supposed to be figuring out how to be in a band without my husband. How to keep my ministry and career going in a new and different way. My moving forward wasn't quitting all I had known to get a desk job. At least it wasn't supposed to be.

Morning after morning I opened my computer and scoured Monster.com, hoping to see a job description that would tell me *what to do with the rest of my life*. Like a job would jump off the page and suddenly become the blueprint for moving forward.

I saw nothing but job openings for a Lice Technician at a local elementary school. *One hundred positions available*, it said. What has happened in our public education system that the most widely available career path is lice technician? I was deeply concerned for American school children. And deeply concerned for myself; I couldn't even be a Lice Tech—I have a queasy stomach.

Days ticked by slowly, torturously. With each new day I began to sense more fully the extent of my loss: my career, ministry, bandmates, financial future, and my own sense of purpose and calling. Each day I stepped deeper into the truth of it all: Addison Road was over and I was left unprepared, unemployed, and empty-handed. A part of me had died.

the
BURYING

11 | AISLE 7 AND THE EVIL SPAGHETTI

◆

Unemployment, dashed dreams, and suddenly finding yourself at home, ten hours a day, with a one-year-old, is a recipe for emotional meltdowns. I had them daily. The most spectacular display of my emotional instability happened on the spaghetti aisle at the grocery store as I was attempting to restore my purpose in life by becoming domestic. This was a terrible mistake. Cooking spaghetti can *never* help you regain your purpose in life, especially if you are *ME*. I am the worst kind of domestic-y woman you will ever meet. And at that point in my life it had been quite some time since I had been in the kitchen.

A decade of life lived bouncing from city to city in vans, RVs, and tour buses will do that to you. Make you undomestic-y. While my girlfriends progressed in their homey Pinterest and Pottery Barn skills back in Texas, I progressed in the art of creating tents for my daughter out of hotel room curtains. We lived like vagabonds. After the fire in the spring of 2010, Addison Road did one final fall tour. Our band went in with another artist on the tour's roster and we rented a bus for the two-month, forty-city excursion. Thirteen of us, including Annie, lived on the bus for over nine weeks straight.

You don't cook for yourself on tour because the food is provided. You don't iron your clothes, because ironing clothes you have worn three days in a row is gross. Plus, where to find an iron? You don't have bowel movements on the tour bus. Ever. It is the unspoken rule that guides every traveling artist. So each morning after arriving at a new venue, we would all stumble off the bus looking disheveled, but clearly on a mission—the search for a *clean* sink to brush our teeth in and a private place to poop. Life on a tour bus is just about *that* glamorous. No cooking, no laundry, no privacy, no cleanliness, no alone time. No *life as normal.*

By the time we came off the road in 2011, hopping venues, green rooms, and time zones on a daily basis with my daughter in tow was normal life. Ryan and I lived that lifestyle for over ten years. Acclimating back to a bed that didn't move while you slept in it and pooping whenever you felt like it was cause for severe culture shock. I literally did not know how to operate in this strange other world. I could not have told you the last time I had cooked a meal for my family or even gone grocery shopping. But there I was in the neighborhood grocery store, on aisle seven, determined to create a new normal. Determined to piece my life back together. Determined to cook a meal for my family, if only I could pick the right noodle.

But I *couldn't* pick the right noodle. Last time I was noodle shopping, circa 1999, there were like five noodle options. Ramen Noodle being, of course, the primary noodle. I mean, it wasn't that complicated: spaghetti, angel hair, rigatoni (if you were high class), and macaroni shells. That plus a few Ragu tomato sauce choices and life made sense. And I'm not sure what else happened in the world between 1999 and 2011 while I chased my dreams, but *my God* we made advances in our noodle options.

Now we've got green noodles, red noodles, purple noodles, whole grain, whole wheat, gluten-free, spelt noodles, kelp noodles, no yolk noodles, and about a thousand different shapes and sizes to choose from noodles.

As I stood staring at the noodles they taunted me. What kind of noodle does a Christian woman choose? And what kind of mother doesn't know which noodle is best for her kid? Shouldn't a wife be able to grab a box off aisle seven and keep walking with her head held high to the peanut butter aisle? And what kind of future did I have if I couldn't even conquer the grocery store? The spaghetti sauces echoed my failure; they were all staring at me, I could feel it. Ragu was judging me. What kind of thirty-year-old lives on a bus, eats from other people's hands, lives by faith, and then goes bankrupt? What do I do now? WHAT? Now that my whole life has failed and I don't know how to be a stay-at-home mom and I don't know how to cook and I don't know what purpose my life holds? Will I fail at this too? Of course I will; I can't even pick out a FRIGGING NOODLE.

And there I was on aisle seven grieving my entire past and future. I had failed at life, motherhood, wifehood, careerhood, at all the hoods. I had just failed. And I sobbed. Deep, grievous, ugly girl sobs on the spaghetti aisle. And God promptly sent me a spaghetti angel. A lady in her mid-seventies with a thick Texas accent, twinkly eyes, and strong hands.

She pulled her grocery cart next to mine and put her hand firmly in the middle of my back.

"Honey, I don't know what it is. I don't. Only the Good Lord knows. But I do know this: Some nights WE JUST DO TAKE-OUT."

She let go of my back and looked deep into my puffy, alien eyes as my lips quivered and the tears continued falling. I attempted to speak.

"I just don't know what noodle to pick out. You know?" Of course she knows. Certainly *she* remembers the days when there were only five noodle options!

"Honey, you just leave that buggy right here. Just leave it Right. Here.

It will take care of itself. And you go get in your car and you order a pizza. Understand me? You go order a pizza, honey, and I'm gonna be praying for you tonight."

And I did just as the spaghetti angel told me.

Perishables and all, I left my cart right there in front of the noodles that were taunting me, reminding me that I had failed at life and had no future. I left it all right there and ran to my car, sobbing.

And that is the day I began to bury. I began to bury the old life that I knew so well and the good old days when noodles came in five simple varieties. Days when I knew what I was doing and who I was and where I was going. I began to bury. For weeks, months, nearly a year, I grieved my losses.

Some people were quick to hurry me along in my grief. They assumed that God had ordained my suffering for His glory and that my grief should only last for a short time before I was back to normal and back to glory giving. But I don't believe God ordains pain and chaos; I believe He *redeems* pain and chaos. And redeemed pain can take a while. Other people wanted to see the bright side for me way too soon. "Well at least you got ten good years out of it!" or "You can finally focus on writing now. How wonderful." Or my favorite, "Now you can really invest in being a mom!" as if I was not *already* invested in being a mom. Their intentions were good, but what their positive mantras and personal theologies screamed at me was *there's no time (or need) for grief; just move on to the next thing.* My spaghetti aisle angel gave me what I truly needed: permission to grieve.

We are a grief-averse culture, which is tragic. And damaging. Grief is a core human emotion; it is the grieving of what we are burying that allows us to fully lay a thing to rest. Once something or someone is laid to rest and we have fully mourned it, which is not the same as forgetting it, there becomes space in our hearts for new life to slowly emerge.

Jesus Himself grieved.

When Jesus gets word that His lifelong best friend, John, has been beheaded and paraded around as a party favor, He immediately gets in a boat by himself and goes to a solitary place to grieve. Perhaps Jesus knew His response in this painful moment might be prescriptive; setting the tone for His disciples on how to process and cope with life's most painful moments. He doesn't ignore the pain and He doesn't tell the disciples that it was just part of God's divine plan. Despite Jesus essentially being on a modern-day tour; hopping from village to village, healing the sick, teaching the crowds, living like a vagabond; He withdraws from all of it to be alone in His initial grief. Of course the crowds of curious seekers, new believers, and zealous fans get word that Jesus has gotten away by boat and they rush to meet Him at His final destination. In His compassion, Jesus pauses from His grieving, teaches the crowd, and feeds them with miraculous fish and bread. But after that? He sends everyone away, even the disciples, and once again retreats to grieve. This time He hikes up a mountain to go and pray. Other times He goes to a garden, or the Mount of Olives where He grieves Jerusalem or the tomb of His beloved friend Lazarus where He openly weeps for His friend. Jesus never dismisses His need for space and time to grieve. And neither should we.

If nothing else, the Christian faith is one masterful story of life emerging from the grave. We are resurrection people who audaciously believe that the ultimate end of our story is life—not death. Because of this we are free to mourn and bury as people of hope and not desperation. And this is good news since quite a bit of life is spent burying. Burying children that can't be and children that are—and are so very broken. Burying marriages, relationships, jobs, and churches. Burying the very things we planned out, pursued, and poured into. Those plans and dreams we thought were squared away. Death and taxes, said Daniel

Defoe and Benjamin Franklin, they are life's only certainties. If death is inevitable, then we should be prepared for our fair share of grieving and burying. But if the words of Jesus ring true for us, that blessed are the poor in spirit and those who mourn, for theirs is the kingdom of heaven and the gift of comfort, then grieving becomes bearable.

It is indispensable to grieve as a person of hope. The death of a dream, plan, or person we love dearly is not the end. It is, however, the starting point on our road to becoming. That place where eventually, somehow, someway new life is birthed. Don't get me wrong, burying doesn't feel like new life; it feels like meltdowns on the spaghetti aisle; it feels like a desert. But the desert is the gateway to waiting. The waiting is the womb. And out of the womb comes new life.

I don't usually make friends by inviting them to a funeral, but that is how this road to becoming truly begins. We must be unafraid to grieve and bury.

12 | DEAD GOLDFISH AND A HOLY SUMMONS

◆

I am in love with Benjamin Franklin. I can't help it. His laundry list of accomplishments is mesmerizing. *Poor Richard's Almanac.* The creator of the modern-day furnace. Public libraries? Public heaven if you ask me. The Philadelphia Philosophical Society. The public fire department and the inventor of the Post Office. Our country's most influential diplomat of all time. Electricity! I mean, he really connected the dots on that one, y'all. Oh yeah, and a little ol' document known as the *Declaration of Independence*! The man single-handedly shaped, created, or invented entire aspects of the world in which we live in today. Don't get me started. My love for Benjamin Franklin runs deep.

I have decided that one of Franklin's most important works is an epitaph he wrote for the Shipley family's pet squirrel. Walter Isaacson tells it in the recounting of Ben's life. Yeah, we're on a first name basis. When Ben wrote the first draft of his autobiography, he lived in England with Anglican Bishop Jonathan Shipley, his wife Georgiana, and their five daughters. Ben found the girls to be absolutely delightful (he found *most* women to be absolutely delightful) and he had his wife send over a pet squirrel from America to become the newest Shipley family pet. Which makes me wonder, are there no squirrels in France? Are the French not blessed with new squirrel road kill each morning? I digress.

Less than a year after the squirrel's arrival, the family's pet met an unfortunate ending in the jaws of a dog. In Franklin-esque fashion, Ben penned a proper farewell epitaph for the beloved squirrel.

In a letter to Georgianna he says, "I lament with you most sincerely the unfortunate end of poor Mungo: few squirrels were better accomplished; for he had had a good education, had traveled far, and seen much of the world... he should not go like common Skuggs without an elegy or epitaph. Let us give him one in the monumental stile and measure, which being neither prose nor verse, is perhaps the properest for grief; since to use common language would look as if we were not affected, and to make rhymes would seem trifling in sorrow."

"Mungo," Franklin told Georgianna, "Deserves something a little more eloquent than such a simple epitaph with such little heart as: *Here Skugg Lies, Snug as a Bug in a Rug.*"

One of the most beloved adages spoken over children around the world at night is Franklin's example of a heartless eulogy for a rodent, a eulogy that would simply not do for the family's beloved pet squirrel. And while this letter is one of many non-sensical examples of Benjamin Franklin's famous use of grandiose words written to enshrine him upon hearts and history, what he has done in this letter is really, very important for the griever. He has given a squirrel a proper farewell. *A SQUIRREL.*

It seems silly, really. Unimportant. Dastardly unequivocal to the eulogies spoken at funerals mourning the loss of people we love the most. But Franklin understood that a death is a death, no matter how small. And I am of the opinion that all deaths should be grieved as such. Perhaps Dr. Seuss' compassionate elephant, Horton, would say the same? If a person is a person, no matter how small; then a death is a death, no matter how small.

No one can place a value on that which has died unless they have loved it intimately first. No one can grieve what they have not dreamed of and cared for in quite the same way as the dreamer and the caregiver. It doesn't matter what the size of the loss is. Things of all shapes and sizes die. Dreams. Dads. Dogs. If you are burying, then you are burying. And burying hurts. No matter what is being buried.

I met an Army wife once who understood this. She was telling me about her husband's third deployment to Afghanistan and said she could do a lot of hard things with him away. Like handling the burial of her grandpa, the kids being sent home from school for bad behavior, the broken refrigerator, and the stretching thin of money that never seemed to cover the bills. But, she said, "When I came home and the neighbor's evil cat was eating the tomatoes off my tomato plants, I lost it. I just absolutely lost it. And I screamed at that cat like he was eating my child."

I met another Army mom who was grieving and burying something much more difficult. She came to me after a show and told me her son was a runner. She had only ever dreamed of him running and had cheered him on his whole life. He just returned from Afghanistan with no legs. Tears ran down her face as she said, "I realized tonight as you were talking that there are some dreams I've had for him that I guess I need to let go of and bury now. I just don't know how to though."

I immediately felt ridiculous for talking about my own grief as it paled in comparison.

But we cannot underestimate or undervalue any grief, no matter the shape or size. Grief cannot be compared. It must be embraced before it can be laid to rest. So whether it is the eating of the tomato plant, or the loss of your son's legs, or a road that has suddenly run out, or my daughter grieving the death of an imaginary friend, it's worthy of an epitaph.

We've all seen TV shows or movies where a little kid's pet dies, they are devastated, and then the family gathers to give it a proper going away. Bill Cosby, as usual, does it best. When daughter Rudy's pet goldfish dies, Cosby's character, Cliff Huxtable, has the entire family dress up in their Sunday best and solemnly walk to the bathroom. With the pet fish wrapped up in toilet paper, he begins the service, "We're here to say goodbye to a cherished friend, Lamont Goldfish." Everyone giggles and Rudy interjects, "Daddy, I want to watch television." Dr. Huxtable quips back, "Yeah, you see, we're having a funeral for your friend." Rudy insists she wants to watch TV *now*. "NOBODY IS GONNA WATCH TV UNTIL THE FUNERAL IS OVER. IS THAT CLEAR?"

When a child loses something dear to them, whether it is a pet gold-fish or a grandma, we grieve with them. Very rarely do we tell a child, "Just get over it." When the goldfish dies, we dress up and march to the bathroom and say what the Patron Saint of Fathers, Bill Cosby, said, *We all dressed up and we WILL have a funeral for this goldfish. Is that clear?* If compassion, humor and careful insistence on closure are gifts that we give our children when they are dealing with loss, why should we treat our own grief any different as adults?

Our daughter, Annie, is a natural-born-griever. She has actually asked me to *not* put chocolate chip smiley faces on her pancakes because she feels sad about eating the person. She grieved the end of preschool for days, eulogizing through tears her love for her teacher, friends, sand-box, and her favorite water fountain. And when a band mate discov-ered his French coffee press had broken while on the road, her eyes welled up with tears and she cried over his loss for nearly ten minutes. Annie keeps teaching me about this universal concept of loss, and daily reminds me that children might be our best hope at recovering the art of grieving and burying well.

When my grandmother, Annie's great-grandmother, passed away, Ryan and I planned to take her to Mississippi without actually telling her that Mamaw had died. We certainly did not want Annie at the funeral. After all, she was only a few days shy of turning five and caskets and gravesides seemed a bit much for a child who grieved not-real-pancake-faces.

We told her we were making a last minute trip to Mississippi to be with all the family. We told her how fun it would be to see her cousins, grandparents, aunts, and uncles!

"But why are they going to Mississippi?" she asked suspiciously. I evaded her question and talked about other things. "But Mom, why don't we wait until Mamaw is better and can walk again and then we can all go?" Finally, and I knew she was baiting me, "But is everyone going to be there, Mom, even my Mamaw?"

She is a smart child and perhaps there are much better ways of parenting, but since I've already started an "Annie's Therapy" fund, all I knew to do in that moment was tell her the truth.

"Baby, Mamaw is going to be there, but not in the way we have ever known her. Mamaw died this morning, sweetie, and she went to heaven to be with Jesus and Papaw and her daughter, Debbie. And now she can walk again and see all the people she loves and be with God."

Annie lost it. Sobbing uncontrollably. I told her more about heaven, and that we really don't know anything for sure. We just know it's where God is and all things are made whole; it's where God's children go back home to and they get new bodies and are surrounded by His love and beauty.

"IF GOD GIVES NEW BODIES, WHY CAN'T HE JUST SEND HER BACK HERE WITH HER BETTER BODY?" she yelled in frustration.

And what a brilliant question for a five-year-old who loves her life HERE. If we are made wholly well in God's presence, why *can't* God send us back here? I decided this was not the appropriate time to debunk reincarnation or explain to her that this world isn't all it's cracked up to be. Instead, I tried to remember everything Mr. Rogers had ever taught me about helping a child express their emotions. I told her it was okay to be angry and sad. It was okay to ask God questions. I told her that when we are sad and angry there are lots of things we can do to get those feelings out so they don't stay inside of us and make us sick. I told her some people color and paint until they feel better. Some people scream into pillows and punch a mattress. Some people go for a run. Some people write a song. Some people talk out loud about all of it.

She asked for some privacy.

I was hesitant. But she clearly wanted to process and I wanted to give her the space she needed (though what I really wanted was to sit and hold her while we both cried). I went to the next room, shut my door, and immediately turned on the baby monitor. She eulogized through tears, "Mamaw, I'm so sorry you died. I only ever knew you when your legs didn't work and your back hurt. I hope you feel better now. I already miss you." Then she grunted and growled and I heard her repeatedly hitting her pillows. Then it got quiet. Later she showed me a picture that was all yellow (with deep, heavy-handed strokes) and a blue blob in the top right corner. This was heaven and Mamaw floating into it. Then came the singing. Oh, the singing. How Ryan and I gave birth to a tone-deaf child who loves to sing is beyond me. But she wailed out all kinds of made up songs about how she was sad but Mamaw was glad. And then her door opened.

I turned off the baby monitor and pretended to be packing. She came in my room and said, "So do we get to stay in a hotel room with our cousins?"

And she was well.

We adults might learn a thing or two from children if we watch how they instinctively grieve the painful moments of life. In their worlds, a whole myriad of small deaths and little pains are worthy of lament and burying. Their grief carries no shame, they will wail and eulogize until they are good and finished. And then, when the sting of death is gone, they move forward.

And that's the whole point of burying; the moving forward. So I am learning to be more like my daughter and giving myself permission to write epitaphs for every kind of loss. Because I am learning that whether I bury a friend or a failure, a squirrel or a fish, the act of properly laying something to rest is the first part of letting go. And letting go is the gateway to moving forward.

13 | POOR RICH MAN

◆

In Mark 10, a rich guy runs to Jesus, falls on his knees and says, "Good teacher, what shall I do to inherit eternal life?" Jesus wonders aloud why the man is calling Him *good* since only His Father in heaven is good, and then reminds the rich young ruler of the commandments. The rich young ruler, who has already shamelessly fallen at the feet of Jesus in humility says, "Teacher, I have kept all these things since my youth." Jesus replies, "Then sell all you have and give it to the poor and you will have treasure in heaven, and come follow Me." And the rich young ruler walks away sad. *For he was one who owned much.*

This story is certainly about money but I think it's about something bigger as well. It's about security and the challenge that Jesus gives to everyone who seeks to truly follow Him: let go.

Let go of your own agenda.

The things that keep you safe and comfortable.

Let go of the plans.

The calendars. The dreams. The assets.

Let go of the need for control. The security.

The things that make you self-reliant and keep you from faith-leaping.

Jesus looks the rich young ruler in the eyes and says, "What keeps you from fully following me? Oh, your money? Give it away then. Bury it. Come and follow Me all the way." At least that's my paraphrase.

The man walks away sad. And I don't blame him. Most of the time I walk away sad too. I just can't manage to let go and bury. I don't have much in the way that the rich young ruler did, like houses and cars (chariots?) But I do have a pretty tight grip on my dreams, plans, and agenda.

There's another story in the Old Testament about a widow who had no one to care for her and very little food left. Elijah the Prophet is directed by God to go to this impoverished old lady and ask her for what little food she *does* have. The woman looks at Elijah and says, "I swear by the Lord your God that all I have is enough for one more loaf of bread, then my son and I will starve and die." And then Elijah has the nerve to look the little old lady in the face and tell her to do as God has requested and she will always be provided for.

Someone reminded me of this story after the fire, when Ryan and I were staring bankruptcy in the face. As I reread the widow's response over and over again, I decided I suck at following Jesus. The story made me mad and drove me toward becoming a hoarder. I mean, it ends well for the poor old lady. She does as Elijah tells her to do and it says "from that day forth she had just enough flour and oil to provide for her." But the thing is, I don't want just enough. I want my Sam's Club and Costco membership *thank you very much*. I want a pantry full of flour and oil! I want a storage unit, a lake house, summer house, vacation house, and I want them to ALL be full of oil and flour! I don't want *just enough*. I want enough to care for the entire block in case of nuclear disaster or zombie apocalypse. The truth is, I'd quite prefer to talk about faith and not actually have to live by faith. So I know what it feels like to walk away from Jesus, sad.

The rich young ruler wasn't able to let go because he wasn't ready to bury his carefully crafted security. He was willing to comply with rules, but not willing to align his life and death and security with Christ. Let go of and bury? Follow blindly? This was more than he was prepared to do. And while the passage says that Jesus looks at the young man with love, He lets the rich young ruler walk away. Jesus never forces one to bury and follow. Poor rich guy. He has no idea what he is turning down.

People who walk away from Jesus sad don't realize they are walking away from a chance for new dreams to be dreamed. Some are too concerned with tending to the dreams that will never happen, guarding their illusions of control, or perpetually grieving the past. Others are afraid. And still others walk away sad because they feel inadequate in their letting go. They have been confused by Christian sentiments expressed from over-zealous-Jesus-lovers that somehow *letting go of* is easy, joyful even! *Abandon it all for the sake of the call! On fire! All in!*

But I've never found that to be true. The times I have truly buried something dear to me in order to more fully follow Jesus have been incredibly painful, sobering moments. Maybe we should expect that our *letting go of* moments will initially be laced with sadness, fear and hesitation; the sounds of grief and burial, not exorbitant celebration. Letting go of dreams, plans, agendas, even our own sin, is after all, a tall order. And if anyone understands this, Jesus does. He understands the deep pain involved in letting go; it was enough to cause the Son of God to fall to His knees and sweat blood. Jesus knows what it feels like to be asked to bury something. He knows what it is like to *let go of* heaven for earth and earth for hell. Jesus understands the person who is *letting go of* with anguish and not feigned, joyful frenzy.

Sometimes I like to re-envision the story of the rich young ruler and what it would have been like if he had accepted Jesus' invitation instead of walking away sad. This is how the new story plays out in my mind:

Jesus, full of compassion, joins the rich young ruler as he sets out to sell all of his belongings. First, He journeys the long distance home with the rich young man and stands in the room as he breaks the news to his shocked and angry parents. Knowing very well the young man may never be welcomed back home, Jesus stands beside him as he denounces his position in the family, his birthrights, and his inheritance. Next they head out to the fields and begin preparing donkeys, mules, and cattle to sell. Sweating and dirty, taking the better part of the day, Jesus only breaks his pace to get water for the two of them to drink. Walking across town, the rich young ruler realizes the news of his *letting go* has spread fast and Jesus quietly, confidently meets the stares of gawkers so the rich young ruler doesn't have to. In the back of the cattle stall, standing among animals, Jesus waits while the rich young ruler auctions off all his livestock; his livelihood. And Jesus, full of compassion, sits in the back of the courtroom as the rich young man signs over the rights to his property, his inheritance, his position in society. They walk out of the courthouse, the rich young ruler only having a few bags of money left to his name and Jesus quietly waits. The rich young man takes his final bags of money and somberly gives them to the destitute begging alms on the street corner.

Perhaps we have mistakenly come to believe that our letting go of and burying happens alone- or worse- under the thumb of an uncompassionate God who would sit idly by and watch His own children mourn at the grave.

But I like to imagine that if the rich young ruler would have said *yes* to letting go and burying, Jesus Himself would have preached the graveside service.

Jesus Himself would have comforted him as he grieved. Jesus Himself would have rolled the stone in front of the tomb and declared *It is finished*. Jesus Himself would have led the choir of angels in a rejoicing song. Because Jesus Himself would have known that life follows death. And that new life? Jesus Himself would have been the one to bring it forth.

I grieved and buried longer than I needed to. Walking away from the life I had perfectly planned out and watched go up in flames felt impossible because I was trying to walk away from it all alone. One night as I was lying in bed, one month into my grieving and still unable to truly bury, I saw the entire story of the rich young ruler play out in my head. The new story, where the ruler lets go and Jesus walks with him on his road to burying. It was the night I came face to face with my own need for burial and realized I was not alone at the graveside. He was there. Full of compassion, ready to pronounce *It is finished*.

It was time. And that night, through a million aching tears,

Jesus stood watch and we buried.

the LOSTNESS

14 | ALIENS AND FAMILIAR ROADS

◆

I distinctly remember the road my mom almost killed me on.

I was six.

It was a bumpy, two-lane country road that brought us out of microscopic Enterprise, Mississippi, and into the big city of Laurel, Mississippi. Twenty-one thousand people strong.

My little sister and I were fighting in the back seat. Melissa always won fights. She should have been born the big sister. She is tough and knows everything about everything, and if she doesn't, she just makes it up. She can handle blood, fires, mean people, and mysterious noises in the house that sound like snakes or robbers. One time we were babysitting some neighbor kids at our house and I accidentally microwaved a metal pot and sparked a mini fireworks display in the kitchen. With smoke pouring out of the clouded black machine and imminent danger at hand, I did what every responsible babysitter does: I ran out of the house and down the street. *Without the kids*. Melissa put on oven mitts, braved the fireworks, put out the fire, moved the kids to the living room, and came to find me halfway down the street. Being my little sister is a technicality.

So my big sister and I were six years old, fighting in the back seat. We were sitting side by side because we grew up before children were forced to sit in car seats until they were like one hundred pounds or twelve years old or almost in junior high.

We were arguing and pinching each other when my mom stopped the car and killed the lights on the bumpy, two-lane country road. I had never seen anything so black in my life. It was the kind of black that makes you see milky white spots and wonder if you still have legs. The kind of darkness you desperately want to get out of because you are sure, at any moment, an effervescent young girl with long, stringy hair and holding a cat will cross the road, look you in the eyes, and cast a spell on you.

"I'm an alien."

What? You could have heard our pounding hearts outside the car. The voice sounded deep and evil.

"I have come to your land to see how little sisters treat each other. We do not like it when you fight. We do not like it at all."

She turned the lights on, started the engine and stared at us, unflinching, a good long minute from the rear-view mirror before she began to drive as if nothing had happened.

We were gripped with terror in the backseat.

How could we have been so dumb?

Of course she was an alien. Of course. There were so many clues—so many red flags about this woman—this so-called "mom" of ours. But those didn't matter anymore; all that mattered was our escape. We had been tricked by aliens into believing we had an earthling-mom and the only thing we could do now was pray and plan our escape route.

Melissa and I sat trembling, holding hands, in the backseat.

The drive home seemed eternal.

Every pothole a portal to outer space, the home of aliens and bad children.

We held each other's five and six-year-old hands with the deepest love and trust ever shared between sisters. Ever.

My mom was brilliant. I will never forget that road.

We remember some roads better than others.

The dirt road leading to Grandpa's farm. The long road out of town. The winding road through the mountains. Or the one where you pulled over and kissed longer and harder than you ever thought you could. The road that takes you to school, then work, then home again. The road traveled to bury a friend. The road driven to see the country. The road journeyed every year on the same family vacation. The road run by foot to conquer the body or pay tribute to a friend. The road home. To your first home, the one you lived in as a little boy or a little girl when roads felt eternal.

Well-worn and beaten into submission but still standing the test of time; roads are memories kept alive. Living, breathing picture albums.

Give me roads and I will give you my story. Potholes, pine needles, and parched pavement bring my childhood back to life.

They smell, the roads do. Just take a drive on Interstate 20 between Texas, Louisiana, and Mississippi. That is my road. East Texas earth and cows give way to Louisiana pine and swamp. Louisiana pine and swamp give way to muddy Mississippi River and honeysuckle. Sweet summer honeysuckle gives way to humidity and woods so dense you smell Thoreau's freedom at Walden's Pond all the way down on the Natchez. And somehow the smells are all saved, bottled up into the roads like scratch and sniff fossils.

My childhood smells like the woods and mud and pine needles and that one long stretch of asphalt. It looks more like exit 33 on Interstate 20 than it does the pictures of me and Mickey Mouse when I was nine years old.

The road, so familiar we forget it is holding us up, delivers us to our memories and to our future all at once. So I memorized Interstate 20 from Mississippi to Texas like I've memorized every freckle on my daughter's face.

Something deep inside me felt anxious to know the way home. In case I ever needed to get back to Mississippi and my parents weren't there to help me, I vowed to know how. Fanatic road memorization never left me. For well over a decade I have crisscrossed America and memorized her roads. Tell me a city I have been to and I will tell you how to get to its center, where you might find a good bite to eat, and what highway exit has the cleanest bathrooms on your way out of town.

From Arizona to Mississippi, from Michigan to Nashville, from Florida to New Jersey and all the way up the majestic west coast, they are scratched onto the earth's surface like guideposts. Reliable, tried and true. Living, breathing arteries. As a little girl, memorizing roads gave me a sense of security. But now memorizing roads only tricks me into believing I *have* security. As if detours never happen and arteries don't stop pulsing with life.

Give me my roads and I will tell you who I am. I will tell you where I have been. Where I am going. And where I will stop for coffee along the way.

Take my roads away, erode their surfaces or swallow them whole in the abyss of the earth's stomach and I am lost. Fearfully, painfully, lost.

After my burying was done and the most intense season of my grieving had passed, the proverbial road that I was traveling didn't magically make a sharp right turn, straighten out, and lead me straight to happily-ever-after land. It was the complete opposite, actually. After the burying, my road disappeared.

During the spring and summer of 2011, the early months of my post-Addison Road life, I spent an embarrassing amount of time wandering around Michaels craft store; I'm pretty sure I kept them in business that year. With no clear-cut direction on how to move forward with my life or what came next, I looked to Martha Stewart and HGTV to fill my days. God only knows how many bottles of glitter I bought that year. Or what that one cashier thought as I entered the store every week, aimlessly roaming the aisles with my toddler in tow for well over an hour, and checking out with an unconscionable amount of Mod Podge.

No longer grieving, I had entered into a season of complete lostness. I was roadless, mapless, and *not* happy about it.

15 | IOWA CORNFIELD

◆

Growing up, the woods were my home. Behind our neighbor's magnolia tree and a row of bamboo shoots was the most exhilarating place for a little girl who was born to be an unsolved mysteries detective. The shadowy, damp, overgrown woods were home to crime scenes and mysteries that only Nancy Drew and myself were quite brave enough to solve. I collected snakeskins and poked at dead birds. I inspected paw prints and determined that there were at least five wolves, a pack of wild turkey and probably a group of abandoned children living behind our house in Laurel, Mississippi. It was all very *Boxcar Children*.

I loved being in the woods because I loved dead things. I think there are some psychiatrists who would use this to assert that there is an increased likelihood I might turn out to be a serial killer, but I simply believe it points to the inquisitive, detective spirit I was born with. While other kids wanted to be on Disney game shows where you could win your very own Schwinn bike or a trip to Disney World; I wanted to be on *Unsolved Mysteries* or *Rescue 911* with William Shatner.

Not as the missing or dead person, of course, but as the Nancy Drew detective that I was born to be. So I devoted myself to the woods behind my house. Some days I brought a notebook and took notes. Other days, I just took a bottle of water and my best poking stick. Always looking for clues, crime scenes, or critter holes, I was a fearless explorer.

For the first ten feet into the woods I was fearless.

But after that,

I was terrified. The most afraid, un-brave child those woods had ever seen. Each twig breaking under foot brought me close to an all-out panic attack. And the slightest movement in the limbs paralyzed me in my tracks. The sight of a real-live animal? Forget about it. I was planning the funeral out in my head as the giant wolf (neighbor's dog) roamed around, waiting to eat me.

The fear was paralyzing. If I wasn't afraid of getting lost, then I was afraid of being eaten by an animal or kidnapped and never being found. My fears were deeply rooted in the security of someone knowing where I was at *all* times. Maybe it was because my mom left me at church or the grocery store one too many times. I was that kid who ended up going to the lady at the front and saying, "I think my mom left me, but can you page her just in case?"

Or maybe it was because my dad was an Eagle Scout turned police officer, turned military man who taught my sisters and me how to start a fire with sticks, how to gouge somebody's eyeballs out as our best method of defending ourselves, and how to get un-lost from the wilderness, or at the very least, how to dig a snow-hole. Because one gets *a lot* of snow in Mississippi and Central Texas. Knowing how to dig a hole in the ground in order to avoid frostbite comes in *reeaal* handy.

I'm not sure why I was so afraid of being lost, but it was the biggest fear of my childhood.

While my dad assured my sisters and me that when you are lost, it is safer to stay exactly where you are and let someone come to you, I always found this to be an absolutely terrible idea. *Terrible.* It seemed so paralyzing and hopeless. Sitting still? In the woods? Waiting for nightfall, waiting to be eaten? Trusting someone else to come and *un-lost* you?

No thanks.

I'd rather get more lost. And be more terrified. And keep repeating the senseless cycle. Anything but sitting in the lostness. Anything but waiting for someone else to come and find me.

The state of Iowa confounds and befuddles me. It's a never-ending maze of cornfields. We *don't-like-to-be-lost* people, well, we don't like mazes. Or cornfields. Or mazes *IN* cornfields. Don't even think about asking us to do a midnight maze on Halloween. Not. Okay.

Ryan and I were driving through the cornfields of Iowa once, when suddenly the road just stopped. I mean, you could see where the road eventually would keep going, but for the time being, it literally stopped without any warning. Right there, in the middle of that two-lane country highway, 150 miles away from the city we had come from, there was a big sign that said "ROAD CLOSED."

Now I can get cell signal at the top of most mountains, but apparently Iowa is off-grid. There was no cell signal. No GPS. No human beings so we could go old-fashioned and just ask for directions. Nothing. Just a mom, a dad, a baby, and a bunch of corn.

You have three options when this type of thing happens. Immediately turn around and go back to where you came from. Or, bump up against the road closed sign while singing magical incantations and hoping that maybe, eventually, by bumping into it enough the great and powerful Wizard of Oz will send a fairy godmother who gives you a yellow brick road instead of cement trucks and gaping holes in the ground. (And trust me, I see how this appears to be a valid option.) Or—find a different road.

The biggest problem that day was that there were no detour signs. None. What kind of sick joke is that? I think it was Iowa's way of seeing if their own people were still inventive and self-reliant. With no map or GPS you just have to follow your hunches. It was like a statewide hunches test. Making sure Iowans still had them and were still using them. But I didn't want to be included in their experiment. I don't like taking tests, I'm not a born and bred Hawkeye, and I don't have good hunches.

All I saw were big, puffy clouds that looked like elephants in the bright blue sky. And cornstalks. Miles and miles of cornstalks. All I saw was a *Road Closed* sign and I knew that we were traveling on borrowed time. Soon the small baby in the back seat would erupt into baby melodrama. I saw stress. Tears. And never ending cornstalks. The whole world could eat from that corn.

But Ryan saw adventure. It was what every tornado-chasing man's dreams are made of. He looked around, eyes wide and giddy. Christmas had come early. He picked a gravel road. And took off. Ryan took off on gravel roads meant for tractors with cornstalks twenty feet high on either side of us like he was in his little boy Tonka truck. Like there was not a baby in the backseat. Like he had driven through cornstalks before. Like we weren't in a compact rental car.

He turned corner after corner, gravel road after gravel road, following what he thought was a "trail" leading us back to the road. I think he was killing time. I think he was secretly hoping for a tornado to come rip-roaring through like it does in the movies. Or hoping his hunches would kick in.

We traipsed through bumpy gravel roads in between cornstalks for well over an hour. He smiled and I cursed Iowans. I figured we would end up in Canada. But eventually he managed to find his way out of corn and onto concrete. He crept back onto the highway, almost exactly where the highway reopened. The man was more brilliant than I even knew. With a crying baby and an irritated wife who did not think it was legal for roads to just stop with no warning, he wore a private smile on his face. Just for him. He embraced the detour and he won. He conquered the corn.

Some people are desperate for a detour. It's a pretty good litmus test for figuring out if you are in the right place or not. If you can't stand your current situation and secretly wish the road you are on would close in front of you so you can take a much-needed detour, it's probably time for a life change. Don't wait for the road to crumble; it might not ever happen. Pack your bags and get going. You have permission to write your own *Road Closed* sign.

I wasn't interested in any of that *Road Closed* business. I wanted a road. *My* road. The original one that we had a map for. So my answer was to stay at the *Road Closed* sign until someone from the Iowa Department of Transportation showed up to explain themselves and cleared their stuff OUT OF MY WAY so I could continue on the road I *planned* on taking.

I will sit here until you build me a road. Take that, highway bureau.

The thing is, I've never been given the option to lay out the roads. The only choice I get is what to do when the road suddenly ends. Do I sit, wishing and hoping that the road I planned on taking will magically reappear? Convinced that if I wait one more day things will change? Sure that if I get angry enough or sad enough or pathetic enough someone will come along and build that road for me just the way I wanted it? Just the way I planned it? Sometimes I live like a hardheaded, delusional maniac, hell bent on my original plan working.

Or do I take a different road? Do I follow an unknown detour?

The frightening, frustrating, foreign detour.

Taking a different road means defeat of the original plan must come to pass. And that hurts; it's a death in itself. The original plan took dreaming, planning and soul. *Plan A* became etched into a stream of concrete in my brain, into the flow of blood in my heart.

Sometimes it disappears so quickly and morphs into a road closed sign. How dare it do that? I want to punch the air and have words with all the high school teachers who prodded me to come up with my ten-year plan. All the colleges who convinced me that by going to *their* school I would come out on the other side with a guaranteed road. All the friends and family and Disney movies that said, "Go for your dreams! Follow your heart!" As if the world always complies with dreams or heart.

Why didn't any of these people mention potholes? Detours? Roads that bottomed out into nothing in the middle of cornfields in Iowa?

I have spent so many weary nights cursing the world for mudslides, typhoons, avalanches, hurricanes, earthquakes, leprechauns, tidal waves, and every other calamity or abnormality that causes erosion to the soil—which causes erosion to the *roads*, which causes *detours*, which causes severe emotional torment in the heart of a girl who did a fine job picking out a good enough road in the first place. Stop with the detours already. Haven't you taken enough from me? I'm so tired. And so lost. And so tired of feeling so lost.

But detours happen all the same. Not because God thinks it's a good way to teach me a lesson or sees an opportunity to create glory for

Himself by thrusting me into chaos. I do not believe God is the author of chaos. Or pain. In a broken world, detours just happen. *Road Closed* signs don't surprise God, but it is my firm belief that they are not the works of His hands either. Still — in the middle of the pain, in the center of the detour, I see God.

I hear a voice calling my name. A prodding, whisper, guide.

"I will give you the treasures of darkness and riches hidden in secret places, so that you may know that it is I, the LORD, the God Of Israel, who call you by your name," says the Lord to the Prophet Isaiah.

Says the Lord to me in the middle of a dark wood and a nameless road.

The road you planned on using no longer exists, Jenny. But don't be afraid; I will give you treasures that can only come from dark places.

When my life intersects with the world's brokenness, Emmanuel intersects with me. *God with us.* The one who knows the way through dark woods and nameless roads—-He will lead me. Waking me at dawn, helping me lace up my hiking boots. He reminds me to grab a water bottle, a flashlight and some bug spray. Coffee's fixed. Before the sun wakes the birds. Before the birds rise and wake the world. He is present. Prepared. I don't hear a word, but I don't have to. His eyes tell me everything I need to know about where we are going; about how I can trust Him.

Following Him in the dark places is scary, but not paralyzing. He knows when we should make a trail and where to pitch the tent. Where the next stream of life-giving water is and what the village on the other side of the mountain looks like. He sees what I cannot and illuminates the path. Not running ahead of me; not forcing me. But side-by-side, as trusted friends, we walk step in step. And I realize I am walking on holy ground. My lostness is made holy, my journey made bearable, my unknowing state becomes fully known as God journeys deep into the dark places with me. He is the treasure. His presence, the riches found in secret places. With each step the detour feels less like a curse and more like a holy excursion. Jesus has become the guide and the Guide is teaching me how to move forward in the dark.

Do you trust Me? I hear Him ask.

My answer is sheepish and small. I don't yet have the courage to look Him full in the eyes.

"Yes. I mean, I don't know how. But I'm trying. I want to trust You."

Then take My hand. Oh, and Jenny? Fear not. Fear not. Fear not. Fear not.

The *treasure of darkness* tells me not to fear. The *riches hidden in secret places* invite me to follow Him deep into the unknown. I am not alone in my lostness.

16 | LOST GIRL

◆

I wanted to be found as fast as humanly possible. This was my game plan in early 2011:

1. Apply to work at Starbucks.
2. Continue playing Addison Road shows (with hired musicians) until all contracts are fulfilled. Until I can acknowledge there *is no Addison Road* anymore.
3. Apply to grad school. Become the diplomat I have always dreamed of becoming!
4. Check graduate school sticker price. Grad school is a no-go.
5. Contemplate working on a church staff. Break out in hives.
6. Reapply to Starbucks.
7. Make glittery craft projects with my two-year-old.
8. Cry over my complete state of lostness.
9. Repeat.

Were it up to me, I would have become a lifelong barista. Not because I dreamed of pulling the perfect espresso shot, but because it was an answer. And sometimes, desperate people will take a *wrong* answer over no answer at all. But that really isn't the answer either, is it? During the spring of 2011 when I could often turn on the radio and hear an Addison Road song—my own voice playing over syndicated airwaves for a million people, I was applying to work at Starbucks. It was a short-sighted rebound for a lost girl uncomfortable with having no answers or immediate direction in her life.

I dreaded looking at a blank calendar; I hadn't seen a blank month on the calendar in over a decade. My role as Annie's mom was not lost on me. We played hard, took daily walks to the library, made craft projects, and lay in the grass counting clouds and catching bugs. I loved every moment (*well, almost every moment*) of being a full-time mom. But I knew for me, mothering was only a part of who I was and what I was supposed to be about.

Busyness for the sake of busyness was not my goal; it was *purpose* I was seeking. But a new, noble purpose didn't come right away. "God, pleeeaassee open a new door. Please show me what comes next. Pleee-aaassseee." I begged and pleaded like a child. But the lack of answers and blank calendar dates kept staring me in the face. The whole world seemed to say, "What's the hurry?" As if sitting in the lostness might be good for me. My favorite author, Robert Benson, says, "Be not afraid to wander and wonder along. Do not fear trying to find your way and, from time to time, being lost along that same way. If you will be pa-tient- and patience is not a virtue in these matters—but a necessity—a sentence or two will be given to you."

I was neither virtuous nor interested in patience. A sentence or two sounded like pure torture. And being lost along the way was definitely not taught in school or church. Self-reliance, fully mapped out futures, and divine epiphanies; these were the things that young adults should strive for—not lostness. Accepting lostness as a viable way of existing, if even for a short season, is not a mantra our culture is familiar with. It certainly sounded backwards to a girl who was desperate to move forward. Yet time and time again the same message arrived at the door of my heart. *Just be lost for a while.* My husband, parents, pastors, friends, therapist, random books I picked up to read, even songs I heard for the first time, all echoed the same sentiment. *Lean into the lostness.* Don't find your way out too soon. Riches hidden in secret places. Treasures in the darkness. Stay. Find them. Be lost. So many voices were reaching a fever pitch and the exhaustion from trying to un-lost myself was evident—so one morning, I gave in.

It was time to embrace being a lost girl.

Time to accept the seemingly insignificant nothingness of the blank page in front of me.

Want to unnerve someone? Make peace with your lostness.

When they ask, "What do you do?" respond like this, "Well I wake up and take a shower, *sometimes.* Then I look in the mirror and remind myself that I have no job, no future plans and no 401(k) account. I tell myself this is *exactly* where I am supposed to be right now and I contend to do absolutely nothing about it because I have decided to be lost for a season. Then I usually go eat a bowl of cereal and watch *The Today Show.* So—*I just do lostness.* What about you? What do you do?"

Horrified! They will be horrified! It is quite entertaining to watch. I once told this from stage to a group of young, twenty-something Christian adults. They looked at me with disgusted shock. Their glares told me everything I needed to know about our culturally engrained idols of productivity and purpose. How irresponsible! What a waste! She's gone off the deep end! Pity and judgment oozed out of them as they looked at me suspiciously, wondering if I was one of *those* people who lives off of the government instead of my own two hands! I instantly felt the weight of our generation's disdain for lost people. And I smiled. Maybe I was doing the right thing after all.

Did it ever cross their minds, I wondered, that perhaps my lostness was part of a spiritual journey that God Himself invited me into? That the abundance of pity they felt for me could just as easily been given to those in the room working jobs they hated, for companies they didn't believe in, simply to avoid being lost?

Lostness is just a season, I told them.

For everything there is a season, a time for every activity under heaven... a time to search and a time to quit searching. A time to keep and a time to throw away.

We would rather focus on the other seasons in Ecclesiastes 3, like planting, building up and harvesting while disregarding the less attractive ones like quitting, dying and throwing away. Our basic instinct tells us to hold on, not let go. Perhaps that is why we have become a culture of *doers* who would just as soon accept a wrong answer than *quit searching* and inhabit lostness for a time. How irresponsible! But is it?

Making peace with my lost state in life happened in small ways. Refusing to apply for a job at Starbucks. A job I knew wasn't meant for me. Shutting down the calendar and not looking at blank days as shame-driven motivation to *just move on already.* Learning to quiet the frantic voice in my soul that kept telling me THE WHOLE WORLD WOULD END if I did not figure out what came next. Replacing that voice instead with a simple prayer, *You alone are a lamp unto my feet and a light unto my path.* And relearning how to tell the truth to others and myself. This was hard since most people expect you to lie. When asked how life is going or what the plans for your future look like, no one expects the person answering to say, "Actually, my future looks *really* bleak right now and I have no idea what comes next and I am a bit scared." This kind of vulnerable honesty terrifies people. Especially Christians. What type of good Christian doesn't have a Jesus answer readily available? A genuine response about faith, hope, being more than a conqueror, and a pretty bow to wrap it all up in? I got the sense from many believers that in their opinion, I was a woman of little faith. Somehow my sitting in the dark reflected poorly on my faith in God.

But I think it is the other way around. A person who is willing to inhabit their lostness has the faith of a great army. People who don't have faith don't allow themselves to get lost. They do not trust God to show up in the darkness and shine a light on the path that leads to being found. A faithless person holds on because they cannot control what happens when they let go. They are unwilling to follow anyone into the dark but themselves.

Wendall Berry says it best, "It may be that when we no longer know what to do, we have come to our real work and when we no longer know which way to go, we have begun our real journey. The mind that is not baffled is not employed. The impeded stream is the one that sings."

As a person of deep faith who believes I have a good guide that delivers lost people to found places, I no longer go the wrong way just to avoid impeded streams. Impeded streams bring me face to face with God. It is where the real spiritual journey begins.

I think back to those years after my dad graduated from seminary and couldn't find the type of job he had trained for and felt called to. Instead, he was working as a security officer at a hospital, a middleman at a halfway house for the mentally deranged, and bagging newspapers in the basement of a building long before the sun came up.

And I think about myself, of course. At home for the first time in years. Every. Single. Day. No constant community. No idea how to raise Annie by myself. So lonely I began to talk to myself out loud in a creepy kind of way. Compulsively binging on glitter and craft supplies. No job. No concept of who I was or what I was supposed to do. No road in front of me, and not able to see anything on the horizon.

The thing is, when you are alone in a house changing diapers all day or working in a basement before the moon gives way to dawn, it's hard to know the sun is rising. Without morning's first hazy beams of light shining in those dark, unknown places, it is hard to trust that there is anything good on the horizon. And yet as a person of faith I am invited to live in the tension of believing that God is present and at work, whether I see immediate evidence of it or not. I am invited to abide in the truth that the sun is still rising. Always rising. Whether I see it yet or not, there's a little bit of morning outside.

God sees what I cannot. He leads where there is no discernible road. He Himself is a lamp unto my feet and a light unto my path. Here at my impeded stream, after the dying and burying, I make a crucial decision to allow the season of lostness into my life. And I put the onus on God to un-lost me.

I get the feeling He has been waiting for me to do this all along. It is my greatest act of faith to trust God to un-lost me. My greatest act of trust to follow the One who sees the sunrise when I cannot.

17 | LISTEN

✦

My mom heard God's voice for the first time when she was eighteen years old and stoned out of her mind. She lived in the small town of Ellisville, Mississippi, and after a big fight with her dad she rolled a joint, had a few drags, got in the car, and drove to the next town over. My mom had been a sex-crazed pothead since junior high.

She knew little about Jesus and even less about herself.

She had no idea she was loved by God or created with a purpose. The only thing she knew was that she was good at public speaking. She knew because her government teacher told her so during her senior year of high school. So Mom entered a speech competition and less than a year later she had won so many scholarships at speech competitions that she was able to go to the local junior college. It was during her first semester of junior college, living at home with her parents and little sister, that Mom got in a huge fight with Grandpa and left the house, hoping to get lost.

She made her way to Laurel, Mississippi, the next town over. She saw the lights on in the football stadium and went in to watch the game and get lost in the crowd. Instead of a football game, there was a stage in the middle of the field. On the stage was a man asking people to put money in the Kentucky Fried Chicken tubs as they were passed down the aisles. Mom watched in amazement as the charismatic man asked for money and people willingly dumped all that they had into the buckets. She stayed to take notes. Anybody who could speak so persuasively that people would just hand over money must be the best of the best.

The man was James Robison, an avid evangelist who preached God's name in revival like settings all over the country in the 70s and 80s.

That night, the story goes, Mr. Robison said, "If you are here tonight, it's not an accident. God loves you and wants you to know He has GOOD plans for your life."

My mom vividly remembers thinking, "If there is a God, He doesn't want anything to do with me. There's no way He could love me."

To which she heard a voice in the deepest parts of her soul respond, "I came here for you, Debbie. I sent him here for YOU. I love you and have good plans for your life."

Mom assumed she was hallucinating, a trippy side effect of some powerful marijuana. But she heard the voice again.

"I am talking to you, Debbie. I sent him here for you."

She remembers Mr. Robison saying, "If God has just spoken to you, I came here for you. Come down front and give your life to Jesus!"

She still doesn't quite understand it, but in that moment, she walked the stairs of the old stadium and went down to the center of the field. The tall, skinny, gorgeous nineteen-year-old from a non-religious family, strung out on marijuana and beer, went down the aisle to accept Jesus because the man on stage echoed what the voice deep inside of her soul was saying.

I came here for you.

That was the first time my mom heard God's voice. And from that moment on, she heard God's voice a lot.

That night she went home and read the pamphlets that the man gave her. They said she needed to get a Bible and she needed to be baptized. She didn't know how to do either but the following Monday she heard some guys on campus talking about going to a Bible study, so she secretly followed them all the way to the house where people went to have Bible studies. It was a little place on the campus of Jones County Junior College in Ellisville, Mississippi called the Baptist Student Union. She walked in, asked for the person in charge, and told the man, Brother John Sumner, that she had gone to the football stadium and heard a voice in her head and became a Christian and needed to be baptized right away.

The man chuckled a bit and invited my mom to pull up a chair. For the next year he taught her how to read the Bible. He taught her the difference between the Old Testament and the New Testament, how to pray, and yes, he was waiting side stage on the Sunday morning she was finally baptized. Brother John was a spiritual guide for my mom and taught her much. Most importantly, that God spoke to His children. That God's voice, through the Holy Spirit, was discernible. Brother John taught my mom that if she would inhabit the stillness and listen; she would hear God speak often. And she did.

Not only did Brother John marry my parents, he flew out to Texas and preached on the night my mom was ordained. Now she has a Doctorate in Spiritual Formation and has led thousands of people down the same road of learning to hear God's voice. I can still find her most mornings with a cup of coffee, eyes closed, listening for God's voice in the back yard. My life is different because of a hippie who heard God speak to her and years later insisted that her daughters listen for His voice too.

Hiking trips? Mom asked us to walk quietly and listen. Time-out in our bedrooms? Listen for God's voice. Fights with friends? Hard decisions? Temptation? Boredom? Loneliness? Purpose? Listen for God's voice. Preferably in the back yard. Because we got the sense from Mom that God talked a lot more if there were squirrels and birds and a few plants around. Growing up, my sisters and I spent a lot of time listening for God's voice. If my mom's childhood was void of spiritual meaning, ours certainly would not be.

From the earliest age I knew two things. There was a God. And He liked to talk with everyday people. So I should be listening. If anyone could help me out of my lostness, He could.

18 | JOSHUA TREE

◆

Jesus says, "I am leaving you, but I am leaving you the Great Comforter, who will be with you."

Here's the problem I have with this whole Great Comforter thing: sometimes I don't *feel* the Great Comforter and I am pretty sure He's hopped a jet to Fiji. I am going through *pivotal life crisis* and He is sipping from a twirly straw stuffed into a giant coconut, white-sunscreened nose, swinging back and forth in a hammock at the foot of the ocean.

I want to find God and hear His voice. The voice that says it's going to be okay and miracles will happen and all things will be restored exactly how I imagine they should be. Jesus on a bullhorn with a detailed agenda. Is that too much to ask? I am listening, but the only thing I hear is the pounding of my own heart. The breath flowing in and out of my lungs. And I wonder where God is. Why is the Great Comforter hiding from me? Why has He left me alone here in my lostness and hopped a jet to Fiji?

When I can't hear, I confuse my not hearing with the idea that God is momentarily not present with me. That He's unavoidably unavailable. All too quickly I begin to believe that I will have to walk through my lostness while the Great Comforter remains silent. But this is where I get it completely wrong.

The Great Comforter is incapable of being silent. I just didn't know this until I took a drive through the real-life Arizona desert.

Highway 93 from Phoenix, Arizona, to Las Vegas, Nevada, is a parched, dry stretch of road through cactus, dirt, lizards, birds, massive rock formations, and strange little Joshua trees that dot the desert as far as the eye can see. I remember the first time I drove that highway and saw Joshua trees with their oddly shaped trunks and limbs, like a million hands reaching up to heaven. The branches of the trees were covered in bright evergreen leaves that looked like swords and tiny desert birds basked in the shade of their blossoms. It's silly really, but until that moment my idea of a desert came complete with visions of Charlton Heston as Moses and the sweeping African Sahara with well-whipped dust storms, bones of unfortunate souls who didn't make it to the other side, and the occasional camel. Deserts meant death, not life.

But on the road between Phoenix and Las Vegas, there was life. In that desert, there were heartbeats.

Little flowers and shrubs sprouting oddly out of parched, desert land. Critters. Birds. Bugs. Cactus. Endless miles of real-life trees. Trees that can grow fifty feet tall, live for hundreds, sometimes thousands of years, and have extensive underground roots. The Joshua trees captured me with their simple beauty. Their very existence astounded me. I found myself staring out the window with tears running down my face like a crazy lady. Joshua trees were living proof that life exists in the desert and the impossible has become possible. God has done as He promised: water in the wastelands, streams in the desert. I knew in that moment, I am a Joshua tree.

The fact that I survive, even grow and thrive in my own desert season of lostness has little to do with my own ability to stay alive. It has everything to do with the fact that I am kept alive and sustained by the giver of life. It has everything to do with the truth that even when it is silent and barren, if there is a heartbeat, then the Great Comforter is present. Is a heartbeat not God's most basic presence? How can the giver of life be non-present if life is present? If there is a heartbeat, there is a God. He dwells within us, we, who are created in His very image.

In his book *The Prodigal Son*, Henri Nouwen says, "The true voice of love is a very soft and gentle voice speaking to me in the most hidden places of my being."

For the longest time, we have been taught to listen for God's voice in order that we might get answers. He might tell us yes or no. Which way. Right or wrong. We come to God with wishes and demands as if we are asking a genie or a magic eight ball to give us what we need. Waiting for the water to slosh back and see the inky words uncovered. Walking away frustrated and confused when we don't hear God give us a specific answer. Our assumption about God's presence is all too often based on whether words magically appear on the eight ball or through a bullhorn. We bemoan God's silence. As if He is not speaking. As if God can *ever* be quiet. The Great Comforter is intricately woven into my soul and His indwelling presence is creating a sound, even if it is only the sound of life beating on in the desert of my lostness.

God is never utterly silent. Job 33 says, "God speaks, now one way, now another… in a dream, in a vision of the night when deep sleep falls on people as they slumber in their beds." I like this passage because it gives God permission to show up in my dreams and gives me permission to say so (which means I sound a little less crazy). If I do not hear God in a big booming voice, perhaps I will hear Him in my dreams?

Perhaps visions in the night? Perhaps simply the beating of my own heart? God speaks, now one way, now the other.

While I search for answers and wonder why He is quiet, God's voice is present.

> I am here. Steady. Constant. Sustaining you.
> *You,* a creature that should not survive in the desert.
> Don't you hear the beating of your own heart?
> Then you have heard my voice.

That's my paraphrase of Isaiah 43. The best chapter in the Bible if you ask me. What it really says is:

> Forget the former things;
> do not dwell on the past.
> See, I am doing a new thing!
> Now it springs up; do you not perceive it?
> I am making a way in the wilderness
> and streams in the wasteland.
> The wild animals honor Me,
> the jackals and the owls,
> because I provide water in the wilderness
> and streams in the wasteland,
> to give drink to my people, My chosen,
> the people I formed for Myself
> that they may proclaim My praise.

Where there are streams in barren lands; where there are people alive in utter wilderness; where there is sustenance in the presence of death and burying and lostness, there is God.

God making a way in the wilderness.

God bringing teeny tiny streams into utter wastelands.

God whom wild animals honor because of His gracious provisions.

God reaching down and scooping out cruel, sun-scorched earth and pouring in water.

God making streams, giving streams, bringing streams—always streams, it seems.

Never gushing rivers of insane abundance, as some like to promise, but streams and springs. Just enough water. Always bringing life to His children in deserts where water has no right to find its way coursing a path and offering up hope. Where Joshua trees should never be expected to survive.

I am a Joshua tree. I can never *not* hear God. If I am alive, then God is speaking. His voice is evident in the streams of living water keeping me alive. The water is God's voice. God's answer. Sometimes God speaks without words; sometimes His answer is simply the next drink of water. So I am learning to hear God in the wastelands of lostness, because to hear the heart beat that sustains life in barren wilderness, is to hear God Himself.

19 | BEAUTY IN THE DESERT

◆

We drove into Paso Robles, California, the day after the RV fire and I remember every part of that little city on a hill. Everything about Paso Robles, California is perfect. Surrounded by rolling, green hills dotted with vineyards on every side, the town reads like an idyllic postcard, a Steinbeck novel. A main street and a downtown square. The real kind of square with a park in the middle, where kids run through soft green grass barefoot, and old men go for walks and first dates share ice cream cones. There are cupcake shops and coffee shops. Shops rich with olive oil and wine, eclectic art and the world's finest foods.

The clouds are better in Paso Robles too. So are the sunsets. They dance through the skies over hills that stretch on forever. Never ending waves in an ocean of impossible green.

I've never been to such a beautiful place in my life. The world can be all wrong, but I assume that in Paso Robles, the world is all right.

When I showed up in Paso Robles, I was empty-handed and empty-hearted. The band had decided to play the Spring Tour of 2010 even after the fire happened. So with rental cars, about three pairs of underwear to my name, borrowed instruments to play, and an eleven-month-old baby, I pulled into this new town broken, scared, and running on adrenaline. Paso Robles marked the first days of my season in the desert.

I think that's why I remember Paso Robles feeling like heaven.

Sometimes when it all feels like hell and you wake up in the barren wilderness, that's when you finally start seeing glimpses of heaven. In the desert, where you are breaking and least expecting to find life, tiny glimmers of beauty take you by surprise. Paso Robles is a bad example, since it is not an actual desert and it is actually beautiful. So heaven isn't much of a stretch. Still, wherever your desert may be, it is your desert.

It's like when my little sister used to live in Hawaii. She lived less than ten minutes from the North Shore and some of the best seafood in the world. Every sunset was an epic ending to another day in paradise, as the skies blazed pink and orange and purple. The mountains and rainforests and birds and waves and beautiful forever oceans seemed surreal. It was paradise. Absolute paradise. And I was so jealous that she woke up each morning in heaven.

But she would tell you, back then, waking up in Hawaii was sometimes a little more like hell.

She would tell you that because she was pregnant with her first baby and her husband was hopping helicopters to help people a million miles away in Afghanistan. Each night she would wait for his call and prepare herself for what would happen if it didn't come. She had more dreams about the doorbell ringing and Army men showing up to tell her they were very sorry than she ever did about playing at the beach. As we walked around the Army base one day, we heard a round of gunfire and everyone stopped what they were doing to pay tribute to a fallen soldier from their base. Tears ran down my face as the gunshot vibrations rattled through my body and little children held their moms' hands and put their own tiny hands over their hearts. My sister stood there, resolute, held together, grocery cart by her side.

"Melissa, how do you do this? I couldn't. I don't know how you do this." And I will never forget her answer. "It's horrible, but you have to get to the place where, if it's not your husband, well, it's not your husband."

And we went into the store and shopped for hamburgers and shampoo.

All of a sudden I realized that even though she was living in paradise, she was in many ways, stuck in her own version of hell. Life can be that way. It might look like heaven, but it feels like hell. Conversely, it might be a forsaken desert, but it is there, in the desert, that little glimmers of heaven begin to make themselves known.

Deserts aren't beautiful in and of themselves. They are painful, barren, and desolate. Deserts are cruel. But within the desolation of deserts, God Himself promises to descend and be present. In physical deserts we see God in stars, weathered rock and cactus; beauty painted against a harsh backdrop. The shepherd boy, David, knew God's presence in the wilderness well. In the fields, in the middle of night, standing guard against predators and completely alone, David wrote some of his most beautiful songs about God's presence. Pastor and author Jonathan Martin says "It was during those long days and nights in the wilderness that David became well acquainted with the perfect love that casts out fear." When we walk through the valley of the shadow of death, it is David who reminds us we can fear no evil. Not because the valley of the shadow of death doesn't bear the ultimate marks of evil, but because it is there, in that valley, that God is with us.

You are with me. Your rod and your staff, they comfort me.

In his description of the prodigal son, Henri Nouwen, describes God's presence in our brokenness by saying, "Our brokenness has no other beauty but the beauty that comes from the compassion that surrounds it."

Deserts aren't beautiful. But the compassion that flows forth from the Savior we meet in the desert is.

I will never forget the manna that fell from heaven immediately after the fire in Las Vegas. As the fire ravaged our belongings and we lost our most valuable possessions for the third time in a year, immediately, manna began to fall. And it fell for weeks. Morning. Noon. Night.

We arrived at the hotel empty-handed that night. It was a casino near the strip that the promoters had booked for us. And perhaps pre-fire we would have been excited to stay out for a bit and play in the big city, but all we wanted was a bed. Thinking back, I'm sure we looked like death walking into that hotel lobby. And maybe that's why the front desk employee looked at us and said, "You look like you've had a rough day. I think you guys need to stay in the penthouse suite tonight. It's open, and it's no charge to you. I just feel like giving it to someone." We looked at each other, puzzled. The penthouse suite in a Vegas hotel? We didn't even own suitcases. We didn't even own underwear. No toothbrushes. Nothing. We were the most broke people in the building. There were no clothes to wear the next morning and yet here we were traipsing up to the penthouse suite to spend the night. I was bewildered at the irony of it all. That guy had no idea who he just gave the room to. Or maybe he did.

Our room had a doorbell and a hallway closet. The living room, with a one-hundred-inch plasma TV, was bigger than our entire apartment. Vaulted ceilings and floor-to-ceiling windows overlooking the city topped it off. There was a guest bathroom for parties. Plush couches.

An oversized king bed in a completely different room and a master bathroom that rivaled a palace. It had three sinks. A three-headed shower with a built-in steamer. The biggest bathtub I've ever seen in my life and bubble bath and robes draped over the edge. There was a separate room for the toilet, and two flat screen TVs just in case the ones in the living room and bedroom didn't suffice.

We invited the rest of the guys in the band to our room. "Please ring the doorbell," I said. I put Annie down into what is probably the nicest bed she will ever sleep in. "Treasure it, baby," I whispered in her ear. The boys came over, and they walked in with jaws dropped to the floor. Luxury lavished upon the lowly.

Earlier that night, Jimmy and Lori, Las Vegas music staples, came to our show. Jimmy had a migraine and didn't want to come. Lori made him. After the show they found us. "We know why we were supposed to come tonight. We are not rich people, but we got a refund check from our taxes that we had no idea we were getting. It's for $1,000. Meet us in the lobby tomorrow morning and let's go get you people some clothes." They met us the next morning and took us to TJ Maxx. We picked out a few items and met back at the register, but Jimmy said, "Now look, I don't want to get too personal here, but you're going to need underwear. You guys go get suitcases, and all the clothes you need. Top to bottom. Don't come back till you have spent that money."

I still wear the shoes I bought that morning. I call them my fire shoes. We got everything we needed.

After TJ Maxx in Las Vegas, we drove our rental cars to Paso Robles, California, and experienced unending compassion from the people there. One lady showed up that evening with ten jackets. She laid them out on a table and said, "I know they may not all fit, but I brought as many sizes and styles as we had in the house. You are going to need a jacket. Take whichever ones you like." Another girl handed me a bag of clothes after the concert. "If you knew how much I loved clothes, you would know what a big deal this is!" She laughed and opened the bag to reveal some of the most expensive clothes I've ever touched with my own hands. Four years later, I still wear the boots I pulled out of that bag. One man showed up with a vintage guitar. He handed it to Ryan and said, "Keep it." One family suggested we use the next day, our one day off, to recover at their lake house. They drove us to an oasis, tucked among the California hills, fed us, and then left us there to rest. Not demanding our time or requiring anything in return, they were agents of compassion seeking nothing but the opportunity to tend to our wounds. I still remember walking the roads of that neighborhood. Those roads calmed my spirit. Those hills were my glimmers of hope.

Completely beyond my own ability to fix, predict, or enable my next step, I was completely empty-handed before a God whose beautiful compassion was on full display in my desert. Our physical needs were met by the Church. The church universal. They heard about our situation on the radio and they showed up in droves. From Portland, they showed up with makeup and skincare. From tiny corners of Maine and Alaska they sent money for us to replace our "stuff." From Oklahoma they called and offered their RV—free of charge for us to finish our tour with. We told the couple from Oklahoma that while it was an insanely kind offer, it was in fact, *insane*. We reminded them that we had our van stolen, that we were in a head-on collision and then there was an explosion and a fire. Three major losses in two years. They said we should come take their RV anyway. We told them no one would insure us. They said come anyway. Against our better judgment and with a lot of reservations, we sent a friend to Oklahoma to pick up an RV from complete strangers.

Our friend saw the RV and immediately called to tell us that we could not take it. "Why? Is it old? Is it going to explode?" I asked. I feared the worst. "No," he replied immediately, "It's brand new. It's still wrapped in plastic."

That RV carried us from Portland to New Jersey. The young owners, who had bought the RV as an investment into their future family vacations, didn't care about the wear and tear or the miles. They only cared that we not give them any praise or attention and keep going about the work God had inspired us to do. Absurd compassion and generosity flowed forth and surrounded us. People sensing gentle nudgings and acting upon them; they were our lifelines, the very hands and feet of Jesus.

We were given much during those days. It helps that we were public figures, intent on finishing our tour, with an adorable baby in tow. That kind of public, inspirational story means we found ourselves on the long end of people's compassion. Others are not so lucky in their deserts. I spent a lot of time taking the over-abundance of things given to us during that season and getting it into the hands of other people walking through deserts. People who would never receive the overwhelming compassion we received. The hand-offs always turned into tears, stories of deserts too painful for words, and prayers. I was constantly reminded that if the only beauty on display in deserts is God's compassion, then the people of God better have their eyes open, looking for ways to express compassion to the least of these, looking to join in God's work of redemption.

Those days in the desert are some of the sweetest memories of my whole life; I had never tasted such unmerited compassion and grace.

And while it is tempting to think that the physical, tangible acts of compassion were the most important signs of God's presence during those days, they were not. God's compassionate tending of my weary, bitter soul was the real measure of The Great Comforter entering into my wasteland. It was as if I was being perpetually held. And I didn't want to be held, as a matter of fact. I wanted to quit and go home. I wasn't asking God to hold me. I was fighting God's presence at every turn. If I could squelch that presence, I could quit already and do something easier with my life. I didn't want His compassion making a way through my desert; I wanted permission to quit.

Still, He showed up time and time again. I would fall asleep sensing that God Himself was physically showering me with peace and the ability to sleep deeply and well. I would wake up and hear the Great Comforter say *Good morning, my beloved.* He whispered over me all day. I would open my mouth on stage, certain I had nothing to offer and nothing to say. Worried that what might come out of my mouth would sound more like, "Follow God and you will probably go bankrupt." And yet, I opened my mouth and beauty flowed forth. Night after night. God's presence dwelled so richly inside of me that He flowed out whether I wanted any part of it or not. Only in that season. Only on those nights. And people responded, telling me I spoke so deeply to where they were, it was like I knew exactly what to say. It's hard to explain to someone that in fact, I *did* know exactly what to say, because it wasn't me speaking. My body was being hijacked and used as His mouthpiece. That doesn't go over real well in the 21st century. I think you get put into hospitals for saying that kind of stuff. But it was true. I opened my mouth and the Spirit of God flowed out of the most broken, empty vessel that had nothing herself to offer anyone. Nothing but exhaustion and bitterness.

God mended my heart through His constant presence. It came through people. Through songs playing at just the right time on the radio. From sunsets too beautiful for words and birds waking me up in the morning with their songs. It came through words of scripture, on a reel, working their way through my soul. Scriptures I wasn't even reading that would come back to me, long lost since childhood, and would remind me that I was loved and that Jesus was worthy.

Those days and nights of physical nothingness were filled with rich conversation with those I loved and respected the most, overwhelming acts of compassion from strangers, and God's constant, hovering, mending presence.

There have certainly been times in my life where all I have heard from God was the sound of my own heartbeat. A barely-there reminder that He existed. Other times where God's words have been firm and correcting. Times where God has stirred empathy, creativity, and passion. Times where God showed up inside of me as joy and courage and bravery. And then there was the one season I spent in the desert. And there in the desert, God showed up as my Protector and Mender. The way my dad stayed up with me, around the clock, after my tonsils were taken out. Making sure I didn't choke or feel any pain or cry out for Him, only to have my whispers fall away into the darkness of the room. My dad propped himself up next to me and stood watch. And that is what God does in the desert.

In my desert, God stood watch. I had never felt so fiercely loved. So fiercely protected. So fiercely fought for.

I remember boarding a plane with Annie during that season, hoping for rest. We had been in different hotels and different cities for weeks on end and I hadn't been sleeping well with the around the clock feedings that were happening. I wanted so badly to sleep on the flight. Annie was still young enough that she slept through every plane ride. If only I could sleep. In a rare moment, I closed my eyes and saw a vision of my earthly dad sitting in his recliner. He told me to come and sit in his lap. Me! A grown woman with a baby! Inexplicably, I walked to him and sat in his lap. A while later, I heard his voice. "Hey sweetheart, it's time to wake up." I opened my eyes and he was not there. No one was there. I was on the plane with drool running down my face. I was keenly aware of the fact that in some sort of unexplainable way, God had invited me into a holy rest. It was a turning point for me. I stopped fighting a divine God who would woo me to sleep.

I don't believe God sent me to the desert for His own glory or for my own sanctification. I don't believe He found joy in watching me suffer the way I did during those days. But I do believe that the moment I entered the desert He declared to all of heaven and earth that He was standing watch and no one else was invited. By the brokenness of this world, I found myself in the desert. By the mercy and compassion of God, I found myself in a profound friendship walking alongside the Creator of life—who brings beauty from ashes.

Jonathan Martin says, "Far from being punishment, judgment, or a curse, the wilderness is a *gift*. It's where we experience the primal delight of being fully known and delighted in by God." Jonathan says that when we step into the silence of the desert, we find God has been wooing us all along, "The wilderness is the place where God courts his Beloved."

When I think back to Paso Robles, I think of the moment where God began to court me in the lostness of my desert. I would never call the desert beautiful. But God was standing watch. And His compassion takes every broken thing and wraps it in His beauty, making it bearable. Beautiful, even.

the

WAITING

20 | MOTEL 6

✦

Annie spent her first Christmas morning on planet earth in a Motel 6 with scratchy bed sheets, questionable carpet, no presents, Christmas tree, or family. This is *not* a proper way for a baby to spend her first Christmas. Unless of course it is the baby born in a stable with cows and hay, coming into the world all humble-like in order to make a point that will forever change history. But my kid isn't Jesus, so I was hoping for a little more than a barn or Motel 6.

She was only eight months old and had no idea it was Christmas. *But I did.* She would not care if she woke up at The Plaza or in a cardboard box. *But I cared.* I wanted to be around the Christmas tree with family, wearing cheesy matching pajamas and taking horribly awkward holiday photos. At the very least I would have chosen to wake up in the quietness of our own home, drinking *real* coffee. But there I was on Christmas Eve in Motel 6, drinking deplorable coffee and splitting the Christmas cookies intended for my in-laws with the couple who hitchhiked a ride with us. *Yes*, there were hitchhikers of sorts, involved.

Christmas Eve day was spent with my parents in Albuquerque, New

Mexico. It snowed and Annie wore a furry reindeer costume. We took cute pictures, opened gifts, said our goodbyes and flew back home to Dallas without a single hiccup. It was a perfect beginning to our daughter's first Christmas. But once we landed in Dallas it was a different story. De-icing crews met us on the ground and passengers dialed their families to grimly discuss the possibility of being stranded at the airport. In the baggage claim area, dazed drivers burrowed under layers of coats, looking as though they had just braved the harrowing arctic tundra to turn up safely at the airport. By the looks of it, we appeared to be arriving during the height of an ice-apocalypse. And as a true Texan, I take ice-apocalypses very seriously.

You cannot base the severity of ice storms in Central Texas on the reaction of its residents or media personalities. I know, I grew up there. People in Dallas, Texas, react to snow and ice as if a nuclear meltdown has been announced. We cancel school. *Immediately.* We run to the store for basics because God only knows how long the ice storm might confine us to our homes. Grocery stores run out of water bottles and propane tanks. We inch along the roadways. INCHY. INCH. Hazard lights blinking, both hands firmly on the steering wheel, telling the kids in the backseat to shut up and pray as we traverse those roads of death. We may not win our football games, but Dallas certainly knows how to do up an ice storm.

So that night I told Ryan I thought we should just slowly, *inch by inch*, make our way to our home, five miles away from the airport. We could try the hour-long drive to his parents' house in the morning, once the ice melted. I told him I thought his parents would understand if we showed up on Christmas Day and that sleeping in our own bed sounded nicer anyway. "We should wait," I said. He smiled his hardheaded smile and I knew what was coming.

The problem with my husband is that he thinks he can do anything. Watching the Olympics with him is the most exasperating part of our marriage. The Olympic swimmers come on and he laughs. *I could do that,* he says with feigned arrogance. And I tell him, "No. No you couldn't." He shrugs back and says with a smirk, "Oh sure I could. *That's easy,*" and I get so annoyed. SO annoyed. I quip back argumentatively, "You do realize you have to train for these types of things? You can't just get in the water one day and *do* that." But he insists he could. He can do anything he wants, he says. Run a half-marathon, just like so and so. Fix the toilet, just like so and so. Hike the Himalayans, just like so and so. Write a novel. Men's gymnastics. Flip a house. He can do it all, including drive through late night ice storms like he is from Minnesota and not Dallas. Sometimes I want to strangle him.

"Seriously Jen, it's just ice. I can get us there," he says as the TVs in the airport blare road hazard warnings and breaking-ice-news-updates. He says as the de-icing guys spray down the plane. He says as we watch the arctic-tundra-dazed people come in from the storm and wait for family members in the baggage claim area.

We pile in the car with our eight-month-old baby, suitcases, and Christmas presents, and leave the airport for the hour-long drive to his parents' house.

For over an hour we slip and slide across the highway, past car wrecks and jack-knifed eighteen-wheelers. With twenty miles to go, we see warning signs that the highway has been completely shut down. But no worries—Ryan knows a side road that will get us there. Of course he does! The side road is a dark, hilly, country road with no houses and no people. It only takes us five minutes before we get stuck and are officially stranded in the middle of nowhere. I am furious.

As we sit in the car trying to figure out what to do next, I see the shadow of a man walking toward our car. "Great," I say in a snarky voice, "Now we're going to be murdered too." I instruct Ryan not to roll down the window. He rolls down his window. The man is frantically waving his arms as he approaches our car. He is stuck too. In fact, he has been stuck in the same place for so long that he is now out of gas and has a dead battery. His girlfriend and their newborn baby are in the car and they don't have cell phone service. And nobody else has been STUPID enough to drive down this road. They were freezing cold and becoming desperate. They were so glad to see us. We were their Christmas angels, he said.

Together, Ryan and the other guy jostle our car out of the ice. We mommas strapped both babies into the backseat and I sit between both of them quietly singing carol-lullabies. The new couple, the snow hitch-hikers, sit in each other's lap in the front seat of the car. They reek of cigarette smoke and their baby cries incessantly. We make our way to Motel 6. Inch by inch. They wonder aloud if the motel will let them stay in the lobby until morning. They don't have any money. We let our family know what has happened as soon as we get cell service and when we get to Motel 6 two rooms are already paid for. I split up the Christmas cookies I made for Santa Claus and give them to the young couple. We go to our separate rooms with our baby girls for their first Christmas Eve.

Christmas morning looks like stale coffee, over-processed pastries, and scratchy bed sheets. I smile as the sun beams through the window and my sweet baby girl makes her tiny gurgling noises against my chest. Ryan smiles as if to say, "See, it worked out after all!" and I give him the death stare. The best death stare I can use in good conscience on such a holy day. "We should have waited."

"I know," he said, looking truly sorry, "We should have waited." We smiled at each other. After a year of fire, theft, and hitchhiking up the highway toward Cracker Barrel, spending Christmas morning with ice- hitchhikers at Motel 6 felt right.

We left Motel 6 and headed for my in-laws' house—and arrived twenty short minutes later. The ice had all melted and the roads were back to normal. Imagine that. While I am grateful we found ourselves stranded on that back road and the subsequent Christmas miracle that happened, I am more grateful for the lesson it taught Ryan and me about waiting. When I think about that night five years later, what stands out is the brief moment Ryan looked at me with a bit of fear and regret and said, "We should have waited."

There have been so many moments in my life when I should have waited. But I hate waiting. I think it is the hardest part of the entire journey. The destruction of a dream is cruel. The burying is deeply painful. Lostness is maddening. But the waiting? *Pure. Torture.*

On my road to becoming, I realized how much easier it was for me to make peace with seasons of destruction, loss, and grief verses seasons of waiting. When I was lost, there was nowhere for me to go. I could accept that concrete nothingness. But once I started getting glimpses of new life on the horizon and possible directions I might move into, it was all over. I felt frantic to get there already. It felt like the delirious insanity that overtakes you on a long car ride when you have waited to relieve yourself- patiently and without panic, but then you turn the corner onto the road where the toilet is waiting for you and, *lose your humanity.* You CANNOT hold it anymore. You are done. You have made it so far! Your bladder has performed at such superior levels! But as soon as that toilet is in sight your body lets down **all** defenses and you turn into a urine-crazed human with full-on twitches, audible moans, and a frightening level of concentration and deep breathing. Ladies, you know what I'm talking about. The mad dash that follows is an embarrassing, spastic sprint toward the toilet. And I think that is sort of what waiting feels like for me.

I have come so far! I have dreamed big and watched as those dreams unraveled. I have buried and thoroughly given myself over to being lost and plan-less. But now I see a light at the end of the tunnel. New life is beginning to take shape and I have enough hope to think, for the first time in a long time, that I might have a few more dreams in me after all. Everything inside of me wants to take off in a sprint; a mad dash to the proverbial toilet at the end of the road. As if I should be exempt through this final season of waiting and granted full permission to sprint toward the finish line! But running fast gives me leg cramps, and chest pain, and sometimes incredibly uncomfortable wedgies.

Who wants to come into new life like that? The one you have fought so hard for; panting for air, with leg cramps, sprinting like a urine-crazed woman trying to find a toilet at the end of a long road trip? No thank you.

I want to finish well—and finishing well means having the patience to wait when waiting is required. Just because I can see new life on the horizon doesn't mean it is time for that new life yet. During seasons of waiting, dreams are growing up. That anything can be planted and then sprout, grow and then bloom, is holy. Sprinting to the finish line only short changes dreams that need divine time to come to life.

In his powerful book on rest, author Mark Buchanan says, "In God's economy, to redeem time, you might just have to waste some." Time wasting is not real high on my agenda. It's one thing to sit still when you have nowhere to go, but an entirely different thing to sit still when you see the place you are headed—so, so close, closer than it's ever been—and yet hear the voice that says *Wait. Not just yet. Give it time to grow. Almost.*

Almost? Don't almost me! I've been almost*ing* for a year now and I am done with it already! I don't want to waste a second more.

Waiting feels like wasting time to me. It is nearly impossible to walk through the season of waiting if you are driven, anxious, money-hungry, detail-oriented, a doer, a fixer, a mover, a shaker, a hustler, an income provider, or suffering from ADD. I can attest to the latter. Waiting stands in stark contrast to the human spirit of accomplishment and forward progress. It requires restraint and discipline. It calls for uncanny patience, trust, and hope. Hope that you can wait confidently and not in vain. My dad always quoted Psalm 27:13 when we were growing up. It says, "I remain confident of this, I will see the goodness of the LORD in the land of the living." I knew Dad wasn't talking about God giving him fancy cars or helping him win the lottery; it wasn't that kind of goodness. Instead, he was talking about a faithful God who delights in walking alongside His children and refuses to leave them— even in their seasons of waiting. A God who sees people through to the other side. The poet David, who wrote the words above, also penned these, "If I make my home in the most isolated part of the ocean, even then You will be there to guide me; Your right hand will embrace me, for You are always there." When I confidently trust that God is near and in the business of finishing what He has started, I can wait with hope.

Letting new dreams grow and fully develop might mean you have to waste time in order to fully grow, fully become. It is counter-intuitive to all that we've been taught. Namely that we can have what we want when we want it; if we buy it, do it, fix it, make it, or try hard enough. *Voila!* Instant gratification. Unfortunately, this rhythm and pace do not translate well within the journey of the human soul. Very rarely does rushing something have a good outcome. To be sure, there is grace along the way when we sprint and should really just be standing still. But the outcome remains the same. A rushed life bears the scars of our impatience. And all too often I am quick to choose scars over meaningful pauses and holy seasons of waiting. That's how you end up at Motel 6 on Christmas morning instead of your own bed with your own Christmas tree. In Sue Monk Kidd's defining spiritual memoir, *When the Heart Waits*, she says this about waiting, "There's a third way to have a crisis: the way of waiting. That way means creating a painfully honest and contemplative relationship with one's own depths, with God in the deep center of one's soul. People who choose this way aren't so much after peace of mind or justice as wholeness and transformation. They're after soul-making."

The journey of soul-making requires that we wait. Waiting is the lynchpin.

21 | THE RIVER

◆

I love rivers. They cut through the earth like mysterious mazes with no rhyme or reason. Buried deep in the mountains and forests, raging and full. Running along the edges of small communities, stream-like, but constant and alive. Dry beds in the heart of summer lying dormant until the winter snow thaws and swollen spring rivers give birth to the land's beauty once more.

Rivers look like life to me. They are maddening and mysterious, mellow and maniacal. I could follow their winding lulls and twisting rapids for days. Wild and cocky, shy and modest, wise and agile, I am drawn to their banks and captivated by their steady mystery. They break wide open with no warning and just as suddenly shrink into small streams and slow dawdles, as if they have all the time in the world to just be. It has been said that a river cuts through a rock, not because of its power, but because of its persistence. Perhaps it is that persistence that feels so familiar. As if it's not going anywhere, so I might as well let it wash over me. Roads and rivers; they are the markers of my memories.

Ask me about the summers spent at my Mamaw and Papaw's house in

Mississippi, I will tell you about playing on the banks of the Chicka-sawhay River; swollen, deep, and murky.

Ask me about my trip through Slovakia, I will tell you of the Danube, nestled beyond the roads leading out of the capitol city of Bratislava. Dug impossibly deep into the earth, the rocky ledges of the banks are dotted by cottages and smokestacks billowing out their warmth high into the mountains that tower over them like a fortress.

Of my trips to Budapest, Hungary, I will tell you of the majestic bridg-es and cobblestone walkways over the Danube, the mighty river that stretches 1,785 miles across ten countries and tells a story as far back as the Romans.

And of my time living in a graciously slow, by-gone world nestled at the foot of the Bargau Mountains, not far from the legendary Transylva-nia Mountains in North Eastern Romania, I would tell you first of the sweet orphans I got to love on. Then, I would tell you of the Bistrita River which cuts through the heart of the city and has provided for the people since the early 1200s. From the Slavic word *bystrica,* which means 'serene water,' the town Bistrita was named. The river is a living, breathing, moving work of divine craftsmanship. When I think of the Romanian people—strong, resilient, peaceful and artistic, I think of their rivers. When I think of the twenty-year-old self who went to live among them, I think of the Bistrita River and how it forever calmed something deep in my soul.

God meets people time and time again in certain places. He certainly did in scripture; on mountains, in people's sleep, at the altar, in burn-ing bushes. And God is still in the business of meeting and walking with His children, whether that is within the church, at the foot of the ocean, on long jogs, in deserts, or like for me, at rivers.

Every year on my pilgrimage to New Mexico I end my time by going out to the same river. I drive past Glorieta and the last bar of cell phone service for a good long while. I stop at the only gas station in town and grab tacos, water and fuel, the only things I really need in life! I head north past the Pecos Benedictine Monastery, simple and unadorned. The word *Peace* etched into their welcome sign; the word *peace* inviting me in. And then I follow the curve in the road and begin the long, winding drive deep into the Santa Fe National Forest.

I always end up at the same spot on the Pecos River. A gravel pathway shrouded by soaring pine trees, a quick hike down, and then out to a large boulder in the middle of the icy cold river. Far beyond the realm of cell phone service or human interaction, I return to this exact spot each year to breathe deep, sit in silence, and wait on God.

God meets me at rivers and shows me something about myself and something about His love that I do not seem to hear, learn, or know any other way. It is here that I am most able to fully embrace the love of God. One of my favorite artists, Nichole Nordeman, writes this about rivers:

> Rolling River God, little stones are smooth
> But only once the water passes through
> So I am a stone, rough and grainy still
> Trying to reconcile this river's chill

I learned to play piano because of this song lyric. I was a senior in high school and the song *Rolling River God* had captured my soul. For months I would come home from school, sit behind the ivory keys, and torture my entire family as I searched for each and every note. No small task for a girl who didn't know the difference between the black keys and the white keys; a girl who flunked out of piano by age four. But day after day I sat there. Searching. Hunting down notes, listening to the song on repeat, listening to a language I did not know anyone else spoke. I was sure the song had been written just for me; the girl who met God at rivers since she was small enough to sit by a stream and cry over its beauty and ache over its movement. Like a prayer on my lips, this lyric has guided me for fifteen years now.

> But when I close my eyes and feel you rushing by
> I know that time brings change and change takes time
> And when the sunset comes, my prayer would be this one
> That you might pick me up and notice that I am
> Just a little smoother in your hand

At the time, I had no idea who Nichole Nordeman was but I knew she understood a language that few others seemed to speak. She knew the power of a river and a God who made rough things smooth. I imagined she and I could hike down to a riverbed and sit on giant boulders, feet dangling into the icy cold current and wait while the water made its way down and around us. And at the end of the day we would be a little more holy.

The place where you intersect with Christ's love for you, that place where you meet God time and time again—-that is your river. At the river, I am unashamed to be me. I am free, known, accepted, and loved. Passed over by a current strong, made smooth by the weathering of water that never runs dry, marked by the beauty of becoming something wholly unknown. Someone holy known. It is here, at the river, that I am most aware of my rough edges. And it is here, at the river, that I am most free. I am not alone. So many rough edges gather on the muddy banks to be made whole. We are many. Stumbling beside one another as we make our way to Jesus. We take delight in the water washing over us and we do not live in shame of our rough edges and deep callouses. If not for them, would we ever make our way down to the river to wait for holy water to wash us over? So we wait for the water to pass through. We are a people of waiting. Waiting for new life. Waiting for water. Waiting to thirst no more. And it is in the waiting that the persistent love of Christ finds us and welcomes us to be washed over, again and again, by His love.

Theologian Richard Foster says, "Under the overarching love of God we receive God's acceptance of us so we can accept ourselves and others; we welcome God's forgiveness of us so we can forgive ourselves and others; we embrace God's care for us so we can care for ourselves and others… Nothing can touch us more profoundly than the experience of God's loving heart."

Unmerited grace and mercy are most manifest when we find ourselves in the place where we finally understand *we need* grace and mercy. When I have nothing left to offer anyone and I am waiting for new life, waiting for water, waiting to thirst no more, the persistent love of Christ welcomes me to be washed over, again and again, by His love. If I learned nothing else in my season of waiting but to gather at the river and bask in the love of Christ, it was worth it.

In the midst of my perpetual not knowing what comes next, I am trying to do what my friend Shauna Niequist is learning to do. "I want to cultivate a deep sense of gratitude, of groundedness, of enough, even while I'm longing for something more. The longing and gratitude, both. I'm practicing believing that God knows more than I know, that he sees what I can't, that he's weaving a future I can't even imagine from where I sit this morning."

When I embrace God's love for me, I remember that I have enough. I am enough. There will be enough. That type of love makes the waiting possible and enables me to live in the tension of longing and gratitude. I am learning that when I have enough and I am grateful, *even in my waiting*, it's hard to feel pitiful for myself. The reckless raging fury that I call the love of God washes over me, under me, around me. In my waiting—Christ be all around me.

22 | NOT REAL BABIES

◆

May 2011.

Fourteen months after the fire.

Six months after my husband and bandmates quit Addison Road and got desk jobs.

Five months into my glitter binges and days of absolute complete nothingness—

my water broke in a parking garage.

I was on a band trip, about to play a really important show. The guys were unloading gear from the van, but I could feel the baby heavy inside of me, and my water broke.

Ryan was frustrated. "Really, Jenny? We traveled all this way for a show and your water breaks before we get a chance to play? Can't you just hold it in, Jen?" The other guys in the band were indifferent. They kept unloading gear like nothing had even happened. Like they didn't notice I was standing in a puddle of water about to give birth.

I was confused. Didn't they see what was happening? Didn't they understand? I was finally going into labor. The baby was coming. *The baby was coming.*

In that moment, something happened in my heart that I had never experienced. I felt like I was in my own world. One laced with more beauty, excitement, hope, and anticipation than I had ever known before. I felt myself glowing. There was a deep joy oozing out of me that I had never known. I could feel it in my fingertips and my toes and deep in my belly. It almost felt like I was floating, watching a bright light burst into color. No one else existed; just that sweet baby and me. I had never wanted to give birth so bad in my life.

Hours later at the hospital I was pushing, sweating, moaning. In so much pain that I was biting Ryan's arm.

And then I woke up.

Covered in sweat. Heart pounding. Body sore. As if I had actually been pushing. Ryan lying next to me, sound asleep. Annie down the hall. The clock ticking in the living room. The hum of the air conditioner gently purring. The birds outside my window. I woke up in the stillness of my apartment at dawn, deeply aware that there was nothing in my belly.

I wasn't in labor. I wasn't even pregnant. And the worst part was that the dream ended before I delivered the baby. I didn't even get to find out if I was having a boy or a girl.

Tears began to stream down my face. I felt such loss, such deep, deep sorrow. What a cruel trick. Why did I have to wake up mid-labor?

Couldn't I just have the baby? I tried closing my eyes and going back into the dream. But it was impossible. I only heard the clock. I lay there broken and desperately wanted to know if it was a boy or a girl. Couldn't I have that much? Blue or pink. Football or ballet. Bloody knees or bloody drama. Why let a girl dream that kind of dream and not get to see the end?

Ryan woke up to my whimpers.

"What's wrong, baby? Are you okay?"

"I just almost had a baby. I mean like really almost had the baby in my dreams. I'm covered in sweat and my stomach hurts from pushing. And you didn't want my water to break yet and the guys didn't care. And I was in the hospital biting you and screaming in pain," and then the tears really came, "I- I- I- didn't even get to have the baby. I don't even know if it was a boy or a girl." I was sobbing. I am the kind of girl who dreams a lot and remembers those dreams; but never had a dream so deeply affected me. My heart was crushed and I lay there curled up in a little ball at 6:00 a.m., mourning the baby I didn't give birth to in my dreams. This is how *every* man wants to be woken up in the morning.

"Well, baby, just go back to sleep and have the baby."

He was startled and confused, but trying to wrap his mind around the wake-up call at hand. I told him I had already tried. I tried so hard. But one can't just time-machine herself back into an important dream. Tears poured out as my soul grieved the taste of what I saw, but could not yet have. Ryan rolled over and touched my hair. "But Jen, we don't even want to have another baby."

"I know, I didn't think I wanted another baby. But what if we are supposed to? I mean, what if the dream was a sign? I don't know. It really seemed like I was having a baby..." my voice trailed off as I thought about how happy I felt. It was a happy I had never actually known in real life, a supernatural glowing.

"Ryan, I was so happy in the dream. Something was beaming deep inside of me. There was this deep, deep joy. I can't explain it. But I've never felt anything like it before in my life. It made me want to have a million babies. I knew that what was happening was holy. Waking up and it not being real; not even knowing if I had the baby, whether it was a boy or girl. I don't know. I feel heartbroken. I wanted to see it."

"It was just a dream, Jen. It's okay. We don't need to decide whether we should have another baby at 6:00 a.m. after a bad dream. You should get up. Have coffee and read before Annie wakes up. Clear your head a little."

This sounded like a good idea.

But all I could think about was the fact that coffee was really bad for the baby.

23 | THE SPIRITUAL DIRECTOR DOCTOR

◆

My soul was frazzled. Everything I had ever known, ever planned, ever put my heart and soul into was upside down. Not just by the dream, but by the season in life that seemed to churn me up and spit me out three counties over, mangled, in a river I didn't know.

So I decided to go talk to someone. I needed some serious soul therapy. Except this time, instead of seeing a therapist, I decided I wanted to see a spiritual director. My mom has been seeing a spiritual director for years and had always encouraged me to go, but I always turned her down, because what the heck is a spiritual director?

Sounded like some sort of voodoo doctor to me.

But for some reason, after the dream, I knew something deep was going on and I needed more than coping mechanisms that a therapist would teach me. I needed someone to help me examine my soul. So I called him.

Troy Caldwell was in his late fifties.

A spiritual director, I have now come to understand, is not a voodoo doctor at all. Having a spiritual director is like having a guide. Someone who sits with you, listens to you, asks you questions and helps you to see how God has generally spoken to you in the past so that you can better understand how God might be speaking and moving within you in the present. Basically, a person that helps you define God's voice and prompting in your life.

I've always felt a sense of nakedness when sitting with a counselor or therapist. Being with a spiritual director made me feel a little more naked than I ever imagined I could feel. You're not just bearing your bad habits, family feuds, or the strange voices in your head... you're telling someone how the invisible, Omni-present, Creator of the universe talks to you. And that's just weird.

"So," he said, "What has God been speaking to you lately?"

I couldn't think of anything. Not one single thing.

"He hasn't." I said matter-of-factly.

"How has He spoken to you in the past? Through music? Being outside? Reading scripture? When do you remember really hearing God's voice or feeling God's presence?"

Nothing. I had felt dry for so long, I was having a hard time remembering. And, I was basically convinced that God wasn't talking to me anymore, anyway. I was outside His circle of trust. My eyes drifted up and over. Not reminiscing; just avoiding the fact that I had nothing. He tried helping me find some way that God was talking to me. And I found great joy in stumping the spiritual director doctor. Wanting to prove to him that God did not speak to me any longer.

"What are you dreaming about, Jenny? At night? What have your dreams been about?"

"My dreams?" I thought accusingly, "Who told you I was dreaming? How did you know?"

I sat there, thumbing the coffee cup in my hand not wanting to tell him; not wanting to know what he might make of it. Not wanting to sound too crazy.

"I've been having some intense dreams lately. For a few weeks now. Nearly every night, I wake up midway through labor, heartbroken that I have not had a baby. But I don't want another baby. In the dream I am deliriously happy though, I cannot wait to give birth to this child. And then? Nothing. I wake up covered in sweat, with cramps in my stomach, as if I am contracting, and I realize I am not in labor at all. Nothing is coming out of my body. And I'm lying there with tears rolling down my face wondering why the baby I don't want isn't coming. I guess I am supposed to have another baby? Only I really thought I was done. I honestly don't want another child. But I wake up, not knowing what the baby is, and I am devastated."

I sat quietly, in my nakedness, wondering what type of judgments and revelations he would pronounce over me.

He let me sit in my nakedness. Tender and knowing eyes, waiting to breathe hope into me.

"Jenny, has it ever occurred to you that God might be trying to talk to you in your dreams? What if God is giving you a name for this season in your life?"

A name? What does God like to call this one? Hell or the lonely abyss? I mean, really, it's sort of a toss-up.

He continued with the grace of the best kind of father and the tenderness of the best kind of mother, the wisdom of a sage and the care of a pastor.

"Here's what I see. A girl who is going through major life changes. A girl who is transitioning from what always was into unchartered territory. A girl who feels utterly lost and alone, and yet perhaps this girl is entering into a season of gestation, where new life is being formed. A season of waiting, a season of... Jenny, what if you are not supposed to have a baby at all?"

I fought back tears as he described every feeling pulsing through my body and soul.

"What if these dreams are here to show you that new life is coming?" He smiled.

"Jenny, what if God is trying to tell you that you are pregnant with something new? You are going to give birth. Not to a baby, but to a new chapter in your life."

Tears ran down my face. Could it be? A new dream. A new road. New life? I had lived in death for so long, it never once crossed my mind that I was on the verge of giving birth to new life. I was just trying to survive. To tape pieces back together. To not have complete meltdowns on spaghetti aisles. For the first time in over a year, as his words dispersed inside my head and heart, something beautiful and hopeful that looked a lot like light pushed its way into the overcast of my soul.

"If I were to make sense of this dream, I would say you are heartbroken because, in the dream, you don't know how it ends yet. You want to see whether it's a boy or a girl. But it's not time yet, Jenny. You are not ready to deliver yet," his voice trailed off. I could tell he felt bad breaking the news to me that I wasn't ready to give birth yet. As if this would hurt me a little more than I could handle.

But I didn't care. I didn't care if I had to be in labor for a month or a year or ten years. The mere thought that new life was coming was enough to sustain my weary spirit. Something new was taking shape. Rooting. Being watered and fed and grown. Something deep inside of me brought to life by God himself.

Of course I am bearing new life, of course. I sat there with a relieved, overwhelmed, completely overjoyed smile. Why didn't it occur to me? God resurrects.

You are about to see God be God, Jackie had said to me a year earlier. She knew what every good pastor knows. Life comes from death.

"You are pregnant," he said. "That's the important part. You are pregnant with something new and beautiful, and it's kicking and tossing and turning. You're just not ready to give birth yet."

Later that night I met Jackie and my closest girl friends on the patio of our favorite Mexican restaurant and told them the news. I was pregnant. They celebrated with me as if we were celebrating a real baby. My friend Betsy said, "Jen, I'm so happy for you. I wonder what that baby is gonna look like? I can't wait to find out sister." We made our best guesses, talked excitedly about the pregnancy and toasted my unborn not-real-baby. Hope and excitement were bubbling up deep within me. New life was on the way.

24 | FAT FEET AND WAITING GAMES

❖

Being nine months pregnant is the longest waiting game ever, mainly because you get the fat feet.

Nine months pregnant, for me, was miserable as a matter of fact. I was so fat I could barely feel my fingertips or my toes. Since I was uber pregnant and traveling, I retained a lot more water than most women do and I got so swollen that my wedding ring got stuck on my finger. Luckily, I realized the ring was stuck on the way to perform a show at a children's hospital. As we drove from Texas to Louisiana, the guys in the band tried to get the ring off of my finger to pass the time. It became a sick contest to see who could get the ring off first. When it actually came down to it, my bandmate Travis was the only one brave enough to yank on a fat, pregnant lady's finger. Jeff made gagging noises, Greggers narrated the event for the video camera, Ryan drove, and Travis yanked at the ring as if it were not connected to my body.

We stopped at a gas station in East Texas and Travis went inside and told the attendant he needed some lotion for the pregnant lady's finger. This is not *at all* creepy. One can only imagine what you must hear as a gas station attendant. She suggested Windex and offered to help. So out comes Travis and Shirley the gas station attendant with an industrial-sized bottle of blue glass cleaner. They douse my finger. The rubbing-the-ring-over-my-raw-bone episode attracted the attention of a lady in the truck next to us. She came over and suggested we try some of her lotion. So we tried the truck-lady's lotion. We are gathering a small crowd of onlookers. All the while my fat finger is turning purpler by the minute and nothing is working.

When we finally arrive at the hospital where the performance will take place, I half expect them to go ahead and take the baby out so they can remove my finger as well. But a nurse suggested an ice pack and some lubricant instead. Awesome.

Several hours later we pile back in the van for another long drive and Travis pulls out the lubricant. I am so embarrassed and so over being pregnant and so tired of having the purple finger that I simultaneously laugh and cry. I think of this moment as a rite of passage for the band guys. We've done every aspect of life together thus far. Now they have to be nine months pregnant alongside of me and know what it feels like to use lubricant to unstick the ring off my fat finger. Through this, I assure them, we have reached a new level of bonding and they will all be better husbands for it one day.

Biting the seatbelt as tears dripped off my face and my husband Ryan was yelling sympathy curses for me as he drove, Travis finally yanked the ring off. We were all traumatized. TRAUMATIZED. Laughing, crying, gagging, and relieved. And I think that pretty well sums up what the last month of pregnancy felt like. Tears, laughter, and quite a few traumatized moments as I waited for labor to just start already.

A torturous waiting game ensues at the end of pregnancy. It feels like March of your senior year in high school when every day seems eternal and you are convinced that you are plenty ready to be in college.

Will May ever arrive? Ever? Because you are DONE already. Nine months pregnant feels the same way. Your body, so round and full of life, waits to give birth all the while you are done being pregnant. And if you are like me, you go to the lady who runs the Nail Spa down the street and say, "Look, do whatever acupuncture, pressure point voodoo you must do on my feet to trigger labor. The baby is fine, she's been in there for at least thirty-seven weeks. Seriously. For the love." Yes, I actually did this and she actually tried. But it didn't work and all I went home with was pink toenails and fat feet.

Sometime life is all fat feet and waiting games.

At nine months pregnant, I tossed and turned in my sleep. And with every movement Annie made in my belly, I was convinced that this must be the beginning of labor. When you are nine months pregnant, every time you pee, your water has broken. Just go ahead and accept your fate. You will think your water has broken and your labor has begun at least a dozen times before it actually does. And then, that time you really, really think your labor has started? Give it a few hours; it's probably gas. Blame the broccoli.

I would lie on the bed and watch the rise and fall of my own belly as she somersaulted her way through the night. That she was confined to a small, dark, wet space like my womb mattered little to her. She made as much of the space as she could. She constantly moved her feet and her fingers, sometimes walking them up to my rib cage and surprising me with her tiny pokes and tickles. And I smiled quiet smiles and tried to explain how it felt to Ryan. He always gave me the impression that this was all a little too Sci-Fi for him. Baby fingers inside my belly somehow turned me into ET. But I so desperately wanted him to know exactly what it felt like for Annie to grow inside of me.

I'm not a loner and I am completely ungifted in keeping my feelings and emotions bottled up inside. If you know me, you know this: I want to cry with you, laugh with you, tell you way too much personal information, hug you, and tell you I am proud of you. Even if we have only met once, I want to share it all with you. I certainly don't want to grow a tiny human being deep inside of me and not be able to let you feel it too. Come on in! Sure you can feel the inside of my guts and touch my baby's hand! Sharing life in all its raw, honest, nitty-gritty is the only way I know how to be human. And I wanted to share this feeling with Ryan too, but couldn't.

He didn't feel Annie's fingers tickling the inside of him. He couldn't feel her toes, wiggling around, her legs kicking, fighting for more space. He didn't understand the rise and fall of my heart every time I thought she was coming. The end of pregnancy was a lonesome waiting game. As much as your partner may want to be there for you, there are places they just can't be.

Waiting games can be so lonely.

The thing about waiting is this: You can't rush it. You can't make it happen any sooner than it's going to happen. You are convinced that the thing you want to happen so badly is going to happen any second. Yet the minutes tick by. The hours tick by. The days tick by. You busy yourself and try not to think about the thing that you so desperately want to see. You try and live like you are not living in-between. Like you are not becoming. Because you are tired of becoming already! You are ready to become!

You have endured a long season of complete change and you are so close to seeing the end, so close to giving birth to something new, so close to the next chapter of life... and yet you are still so pregnant. All that is within you wants to rush the un-rushable.

I am so good at rushing the un-rushable. It's like my super power.

When I was in the sixth grade, I got caught up in a marital misunderstanding between my mom and dad. It was probably my fault. And by probably, I mean completely.

Dad was getting Mom a body pillow for Christmas. You know, one of those four feet long pillows that makes it feel like there is a third human in the bed with you? It was a really nice present (in my opinion). It was big AND it came from Sam's Club and not Wal-Mart. So, you know, it was the real deal. This gift was epic. I couldn't wait for mom to get it. Sure there were other presents that year, nicer presents, but in my sixth grade mind, this topped the cake. She was going to freak out when she found something besides my sisters and I in bed with her in the middle of the night.

I cracked under the pressure of waiting. I started to worry. What if Dad's present is SO amazing that Mom ends up looking like a terrible mom because she didn't buy him anything *big* and amazing?

I swore my mom to secrecy and then told her, "Look, he got you something *really big* and really nice. I just don't think you got him enough because his present, is, you know, *reeaally* big."

She panicked. What on earth had he gotten her? As a grown adult, I now realize she was probably envisioning the TV commercial of the new Lexus with the bright red bow on it. Not a four-foot long body pillow. After work that day, she piled my sisters and me in the car. She hadn't bought Dad a big enough gift. She was off to remedy that.

Christmas morning was a total bust. There was no Lexus or diamond ring or new kitchen appliance for that matter. While my mom opened her *big* gift and was excited for it, Dad sat bewildered in front of a mounting stack of gifts: a new leather jacket (back when they were super cool; I promise), a police scanner for the house, and artwork from his favorite painter.

"Wow! You guys went overboard this year. Debbie, *you should NOT have spent this kind of money.*"

"Well," my mom said, "the girls told me you had gotten me a really, *really* big present. And I wanted to make sure I had gotten you enough gifts if you were giving me something big and special."

I think they both rolled their eyes and laughed. They made fun of me, and laughed some more. I hope Dad went and got Mom something really nice. I don't remember. But we had a pretty awesome inside family joke about *that one Christmas that Dad got Mom the really big gift.*

I was just old enough to take responsibility. And I knew this blunder was a doozy. I still feel my stomach turn and cringe when I think about it. While the moral of the story is, *don't tell someone else they are getting a big present if the present is simply big in size*, the bigger lesson of the moment remains written on my heart. Don't rush. Wait.

Wait when the tension makes your heart beat fast.

Wait when it's not your place to step in and break the news.

Wait when your good intentions are only to help.

Wait when you can't bear to see someone fail.

Wait when you just want answers, when you just want to jump, when you can't stand still another second longer.

Wait.

Our aversion to patience, our propensity to hurry along the person who is waiting and preparing, speaks deeply to the state of our hasty, risk-averse souls. We would rather put someone out of their supposed misery than sit through the misery with them while they wait. We would rather cut short their time of growth in order to wrap up their tense moments of untold waiting with a pretty bow.

We like short cuts and quick answers. Happy endings that don't have to be fought for. That don't require mountains to climb and valleys to languish in before getting to the finish line. Watching someone else wait is like watching a slug die. Brutal. Tie that in with the threat of failure as the end result and we almost can't bear it.

Waiting for Christmas morning, wondering whether Mom had gotten enough gifts for Dad, waiting for the whole thing to implode, drove me to near insanity. I had to take matters into my own hands. I didn't want anyone to get hurt. We cannot bear to watch someone walk through his or her own season of waiting. Something in us longs to fix it. Longs to make it go away. Longs to hurry it, rush it, and sterilize it from all possible shortcomings.

Never mind that the wait might be exactly what is needed. Whamo, presto, fix it.

The problem is, when we insist on fixing it, when we insist on hasty answers, shortcuts and *pull yourself up by the bootstraps* and *just move on already* answers, we rob another person of their own season of becoming. Because to truly become something new one must experience the unraveling, the burying of the unraveled thing, the lostness of the ensuing desert, and the holy waiting that happens as new life finds its way up from under the soil and into the earth.

I have a friend who owns a flower shop. I have never spent much time around plants or flowers and of the two potted plants I have tried to keep alive in my life I've killed both. We recently spent a few days helping her move her flower studio across town and I was amazed by the science behind her art. On one long table there were a few dozen potted seedlings in a row that were covered by an enormous plastic tarp.

I thought surely this would kill them and maybe I should suggest she not suffocate them since I was clearly an expert on keeping vegetation alive. But as she explained the different plants in the room I learned that there are many ways to manipulate a plant into growing while indoors. Using a tarp is just one of the many things she does to carefully cultivate the plants' growth. And there I was trying to strip it of its growth! We humans are like that. We see a tarp hovering over not-yet-born flowers and assume it needs to be ripped off. It doesn't occur to us that perhaps they are waiting under the tarp for a reason. Incubating, growing, becoming. It is not a curse. It is a blessing. They are being lovingly tended to in their most crucial, in-between season. A novice might kill them by unveiling them too early, but a true gardener will help them bloom in due time.

For better or worse, the way of waiting is often God's answer. So many people in the Bible waited on Jesus or God or the Holy Spirit. Paul and Blind Bartimaeus, John the Baptist, Peter, Abraham, Isaiah, David, Sarah, Job... even Jesus himself waited on God. Don't over think that one; it will send your brain into a tizzy. Scripture, if nothing else, is the universal story of a people in waiting. "When important times of transition came for Jesus, he entered enclosures of waiting: the wilderness, a garden, the tomb. Jesus' life was a balanced rhythm of waiting on God and expressing the fruits of that waiting," Sue Monk Kidd reflects.

It's the story of humanity. The story of scripture. Waiting for Messiah. Waiting for babies. Waiting for death. Waiting for rain. Waiting for the end of plagues. Waiting on freedom from slavery. Waiting on Jesus. Waiting on new elected officials and new kings. Waiting on best friends and lovers and lost children and lost sheep and little boys who show up with a few measly fish and some bread or a slingshot and a few rocks and change the world. "God uses various tools to conform us to the image of Christ. Waiting is one of His most often used tools," *A. W. Tozer says.* You might as well get used to it. Good things come to those who wait and the wait is inevitable.

The formation of new life is holy. How can it be a curse to wait if waiting produces new life?

Waiting is sacred because new life is sacred.
Pull up a chair then, grab a book, and get comfortable.
New life blooms in due time.

25 | GROWING SOMETHING NEW

◆

I read all the books about how to be a good pregnant woman when I got pregnant with Annie. *What to Expect When You're Expecting. What to Expect the First Year. Reflections on Motherhood.* All kinds of books. I signed up for the online calendar and paid special attention to the size of fruit the baby was in my womb each week. I'd take an avocado, an orange, or a mango in my hand and I would study it. My baby is a little tiny ball of avocado this week. She is a furry mango.

Then I would eat her.

It weirded me out the way that communion weirds me out. You take that little wafer and rub it between your fingers thinking of all the things Jesus did for you and then you eat Him. And that's what I did each week with Annie.

I studied a mango and then I ate it. An avocado and I ate it. A banana. A melon. A pineapple. And each time I took a bite of fruit, I felt a twinge of guilt.

Why would they tell me my baby is a fruit that I would later crave and want to eat?

During those nights my thoughts ran rampant. My dreams were nightmarish roller coasters of the best and worst case scenarios for my labor and my little girl. Growing something new was impossibly, emotionally complicated. And by the end of it all I was worried that I was going to be a cannibal and eat my newborn or at the very least not have enough courage to birth her into the world and just make her stay inside of me.

Being pregnant was as close to being insane as I've ever been.

Giving up hot baths was the hardest part of pregnancy. No, giving up wine was. No, giving up sleeping on my belly. It's all a toss-up.

Being pregnant is a constant journey of giving up, and giving up, and throwing up, and then giving up some more. The entire process is all about making you less selfish. Showing you how to uncurl your tightly held grip on the rights to your own life.

Becoming something new always requires the burying of one's selfishness.

And the whole thing about giving up scalding hot baths, wine, sleeping on your belly, well, my friend, welcome to the most revealing season of your life. You literally get to stare your own selfishness in the face every single day.

Becoming a parent is the most humbling, selfless experiment in the world. There is something in us that fiercely loves and protects our babies in a way no one else ever will. And still, while we are fighting for those babies with all we have, to give them everything we have, we are aware of the cost. Every day I look at my daughter and sense myself beginning to be-grudge something I am giving up or sacrificing in order to love her in the way that I am compelled to love her. It is a strange battle within me. Parenthood is a constant battle to give up parts of you in order that something else might flourish. Parenthood is sacrifice, compromise, and letting go. It is the process of becoming un-selfish, even if you never had a clue you were selfish in the first place.

Pregnancy gives you a small glimpse of what motherhood is like. It's your first wake up call. You feel the flutter and kick of that sweet baby in your stomach. You will sing to her or read to him or dream out loud or pray over your belly and you will be deliriously in love with this little thing inside you that swims around like a tadpole.

Then, in the very next breath you will curse the child and decide that you WILL drink a glass of wine and you WILL have coffee and you WILL take a hot bath and you WILL eat deli meat because it's your life and you want it all back now.

For me, to be a mother is to be as near to the heart of Paul in Romans 7 as humanly possible; I do what I do not want to do and I find it hard to do that which my spirit says I should do. We battle ourselves. I battle myself. When it comes to being free, I am my own worst enemy. I wrestle with Christ and come up selfish and bitter and unable to do what my innate nature longs to do. But then, with His very breath breathed into me, I am capable. I am beautifully awakened to selflessness; I possess a depth of love like I have never known. It's what being a parent is all about. Dying to self.

Letting go of hot baths to create a little image of Christ himself. And one day the hot baths will come back and the one who gets into that bathtub will no longer be a selfish girl, but a woman who knows the pain and sacrifice of loving.

And that's the thing. The whole growing-something-new business is all about pain and sacrifice. It is letting go and letting go and letting go.

My in-between season looked a lot like this. Some days I was ready to take on the new growth. The next, I was begging for the old world, the one that I didn't like but *at least I knew*. The next day I was simply convinced that I was never convinced of anything in the world to begin with. The next day I was in bed. Consuming massive quantities of Ben and Jerry's Cherry Garcia ice cream and talking out loud to the pretty, happy, rich people on the TV screen that I despised more than ever. The next day? I would make a go of it all over again.

Feeling the smallest sense of hope and excitement that I desperately wanted to squash, because odds are it was false hope, I would get out of bed, curse the carton of ice cream, apologize to the pretty, happy, rich people on the screen, and decide to let go and follow the guide into the next space. And then the next. And the next.

Waiting is a season marked by the unknown. Curiosity abounds. Excitement fights to shine through. Fear and self-doubt dominate. The kind of self-doubt that hits you over the head at the beginning of puberty, leaving you rattled and insecure, lost and overwhelmed. The possibility of giving birth to a new person is both terrifying and exhilarating. And you realize, waiting is not just an exercise for the sake of learning patience, waiting is for the sake of letting something grow. Learning patience along the way is simply a bonus. We wait because things grow. We wait because there is a bigger issue at hand than just *what will I do next*, but rather, *who will I be when I finally get there?* Or as author Frederick Schmidt says, "Who am I before God and what am I becoming?"

During the season of waiting it became clear to me that I was just an incubator for something growing inside of me. Are we all little incubators? I spent months seeing so many things pregnant with life that it became a type of scavenger hunt to see what I might find next. I could nearly always tell if a woman was pregnant, whether she had told anyone or not. My intuition toward spotting new life growing was uncanny. Outside our apartment window a bird made a nest and laid four eggs. This only became humorous after I had the light bulb moment that I myself was nesting something in my soul. Annie and I went searching for other bird's nests because I found it rather strange that a bird would camp out by my bedroom window to have babies. We didn't find a single nest in our whole apartment complex. Night after night I would dream about being pregnant and wake up hoping the darn birds had hatched already; as if their hatching would be the gateway to mine.

My husband was really worried the birds would hatch and then be eaten by a dog or thrown around by a neighbor kid. He would always say, "Jen, you know a lot of birds don't make it after they're born. I just want you to be prepared for that. If these birds die, that doesn't mean you are going to give birth to something that dies too. It just means, well you know, birds die."

My world became inundated with writings, people, scripture, movies, even critters who were pregnant with new life, but not yet in labor. It was as if God were out to prove some master lesson that *all things must endure being nine-months-pregnant before laboring and giving birth to something new.*

My soul was nine months pregnant. My life was nine months pregnant. My future was nine months pregnant. Waiting for labor to begin, and becoming a little less selfish along the way. Waiting to give life to something new. Anticipating.

the
BECOMING

26 | OVERRATED

◆

I don't enjoy watching movies. There. I said it.

I don't like movies. I don't!

If given the choice, I would rather be outside hiking, sitting around a table sharing good food and conversation with friends, or reading a book in bed. Movie watching is not high on my list of priorities. If I must watch one, I'd prefer it to be because I am stuck at home with fever and a snotty nose. Even then, I will probably have a magazine in my hand at the same time so I don't become too invested. And that's the problem. I. Am. Invested. Watching movies, like everything else in my life, is an emotional endeavor. After the credits roll I am usually a snotty mess of tears, ready to take up arms and fight a militia, or still laughing over jokes from the first scene. And of course, I want to talk about it all.

Ryan doesn't like this. One of his biggest pet peeves in life is people who immediately analyze the movie *for the whole world to hear* as they walk out of the theatre. He likes to wait and process the movie in the car, not giving any emotional indication to our fellow patrons about whether the movie made us laugh or cry. I find this infuriating. At the end of a good movie, I want the whole audience to stand to their feet, applaud and give each other handshakes and hugs as we acknowledge the movie's brilliant ending! But this gets me to the real reason I don't like going to the movies. I don't like how most movies end.

One time I paid money to watch Tom Hanks survive a plane crash, spend nine years on a deserted island, fight his way back out to sea, go nearly insane at the loss of his best friend Wilson, (a volleyball, which left even grown men weepy) and finally get rescued, only to find out his one true love had gotten married and there were now cell phones. As the credits roll Tom Hanks stands pensively at a crossroads debating his uncharted future. Ryan thought it was a brilliant ending. But I sat there dumbfounded. Listen up Hollywood: I don't have enough emotional energy to dream up my *own* endings, much less yours. Give it to me all figured out, with a bow and a happily-ever-after please. Because if I am going to sit down and watch something for ninety-five minutes, I need it to end properly. *My* kind of properly. No guessing games, mystery, or poetic *interpret-it-yourself* endings. I like a movie that ends with snapshots on the screen during the credits; still shots complete with subtitles telling you *exactly* what happened next and how the characters' lives all worked out. "Jack and Jill got married. Had three babies. Traveled the world and died peacefully in their sleep at age eighty-seven." Ahhhh and thank you. An ending I can live with.

Wrap it up in a pretty bow. I don't care how cheesy, inartistic or unrealistic it is. Give me a happy ending with no question marks. This is the kind of movie I want, because truth be told, this is the kind of life I want. Everything in me longs for happy endings and pretty bows; a life without question marks.

My pastor friend Jackie had some thoughts about how my movie might end. I swear they were some of the worst thoughts a pastor has ever offered up to me.

We were sitting in her living room one night when she asked, "What do you want God to do?"

Translation: How do you want this to end? What answer are you looking for? Where do you hope God shows up and makes Himself known in your story? Our community was big on story and big on God showing up in the story. And I knew what the happily-ever-after of my story should look like.

I spoke without hesitation, that I wanted money.

I didn't need to be rich. Or even upper-middle class. I just wanted enough money to pay the bills. The lack of money issues would give me the freedom to focus on my music and writing and loving people well. Things I felt created to do. I just wanted to go a month without secretly trying to sell my fancy china or wedding ring on Craigslist. For a while, my only prayer had been, *God I want to be financially restored. I want to be the kind of grown woman who can pay the bills at the end of each month.* Not big bills for fancy cars or even a house. Just rent on the apartment and insurance. Not the lottery, just wiggle room. I told Jackie that was how the movie was supposed to end for us.

The picture book at the end of my movie would reveal snapshots of a couple who came home to a cute, little house. There would be pictures scrolling through the credits of grown-up cars and a house full of sparkling appliances and fancy dishes that didn't live in fear of being sold on EBay in order to make ends meet. The big red bow was money. And money, deep down, meant security. That was the happily-ever-after that I really wanted. A safe and secure way to live out the rest of my days, completely void of ever having to truly trust God for my manna again. Because the whole 'trusting God for manna' bit? Been there, done that, got the T-shirt. Lesson learned, humility taught. Now let's move on to, say, learning the gift of hospitality or generosity with my new-found exorbitant wealth, shall we?

My pastor's voice broke in, *"Jenny, what if you never have money?"*

You could literally feel the air being sucked from the room. My husband looked down at his feet. Jackie's husband, Steve, looked at us with compassion in his eyes as if he knew we were being confronted all over again with the letting go, the death, the burying of it all. I was filled with anger. I still remember feeling physically angry when she spoke those words. Ryan just felt sad. It had never occurred to us that it might always be this way.

"What if you never have money, Jenny? What if for the rest of your life, you live paycheck to paycheck? What if each month you find yourself wondering if you can pay the bills or not? Then what?"

I was crushed. I wanted God to swoop in, intervene and bring what I really needed and wanted the most to pass. Wouldn't God get more glory if this story could be wrapped up with a big, shiny, red bow? Wouldn't it be amazing to get to the other side of the loss of my finances and my career and be able to say, like Job did, I've been restored over and again? I thought the happy ending would come when the finances were resolved, the career was restored and I got back to chasing the same dreams, perhaps, in a nicer car. Problems solved and pathways made straight and big shiny red bows stuck onto my happily-ever-after.

Weren't these the things a good pastor should scripturally promise me? Abundance and restoration and prosperity! Didn't God want me prosperous?

If I were a pastor, I would hand this answer out like candy to any broken, hurting person who walked through my office doors or sat in my sanctuary. If I ran a game show, I'd do the same thing. I would rig the wheel. Anyone who spun my wheel-of-fortune would land on the bonus spot AND get the dream vacation to the Fiji Islands. There would be no Bankrupt, double-or-nothings, or blank spots on my wheel; only happy, predictable endings. Good thing I'm not a pastor or a game show host.

I believe God is all-powerful, holy and completely sovereign. He can do anything He wants whenever He wants. But that sovereignty, in my life, has always played out in a chorus of free will, sin and the state of brokenness in which we live as humans. That means sometimes I see God show up in profound and divine ways. And other times, I can't see God's hand changing or shaping the situation at all; I only feel God's presence standing strong with me as I endure it. It's very Psalm 23: *Even though I walk through the valley of the shadow of death, your perfect love is casting out fear.* The valley doesn't disappear and sometimes the healing doesn't happen in the broken body, but the presence of God draws near. The constant presence of God, leading me with His very Spirit, which is capable of overcoming and dwelling in a peace that passes any understanding. Peace that comes without all the answers and shiny red bows.

My friend Jennie Allen says it well in her book, *Anything.* "The story is just not over yet. All the battles aren't fought and tied up with pretty little bows. God is still blowing through this world on a mission, securing his people, establishing his kingdom, reconciling the hurt and the damage the enemy has caused."

Jackie was speaking the hard words that good pastors speak. She was reminding me that I would *never* find the ending I was looking for here, because the story is not over yet. She was asking me to wrestle with what every saint must wrestle with. If God doesn't step in and divinely change where I find myself on this piece of broken earth, do I still trust Him? Can I still live my story well? Perhaps an answered prayer is not the answer after all.

Perhaps Jesus Himself is the only answer we will ever get. The living, breathing embodiment of all things being made new in the midst of a really jacked up, broken world. The Bible, if nothing else, is the most epic story of redemptive beauty ever written.

But even with Jesus, the redemptive beauty didn't come the way the Jewish people thought it would; all battle cry and king-like. The beginning and ending of Jesus' life didn't come how anyone expected, with pretty bows and happily-ever-afters. His story, all backwards, has surprised people ever since.

My favorite retelling of the story of Jesus comes from a wild bunch of unruly, unchurched siblings in the beloved children's book, *The Best Christmas Pageant Ever*. The Herdmans were the worst kids in the whole history of the world and yet when they finally came face to face with the story of Jesus they were appalled that Mary was sent to the barn and Jesus was wrapped up in dirty sheets and stuck in a feeding trough (much like their little sister Gladys, whom they stuck in a bureau drawer). Once learning about this completely backwards story, the Herdmans spent their time in church trying to re-write the Christmas pageant.

"You would have thought the Christmas story came right out of the FBI files, they got so involved in it: wanted a bloody end to Herod, worried about Mary having her baby in a barn, and called the Wise Men a bunch of dirty spies. And they left the first rehearsal arguing about whether Joseph should have set fire to the inn, or just chased the innkeeper into the next country."

The answer God gave us was Jesus. And Jesus came as a defenseless baby to a young, poor, unmarried couple in the dark of night. Why should our answers look any different? More often than not, the story works itself out like Jesus, all backwards, without shiny bows and the happily-ever-after we originally dreamed up.

Jackie was right. I am no longer grieving, burying and wandering through the wilderness. New life has come. But we still struggle to pay the bills. Maybe we always will. And that's okay. Maybe my restoration has nothing to do with money or security. Maybe God is in the business of restoring in ways that are completely other. Maybe the answer isn't ever getting the answer, but getting the Savior. Emmanuel, God with us. The Way, the lamp unto my feet and light unto my path, the One who is teaching me joy, peace, and purpose in the midst of my broken pieces of earth.

Once we have arrived, with answers in hand and pretty bows, we no longer feel the urgent need to abide in the rich nourishment and companionship of the Savior. And what a loss it would be to give up rich companionship with God because I "arrive" and no longer find myself in need of the vine. I like it this way, the not-quite-arrived way. It is here that I have learned how to live alongside Christ—free and full.

If I have come to know anything new during this season of becoming, it is this: More often than not, we do not get the answer we want. It is in the midst of those less-than-perfect endings that my pastor's question stands as a stark call to faith.

Can I live my story well even if _____ doesn't happen?

Happily-ever-after is over rated. The frayed pieces of dreams and unanswered prayers are reminders that sometimes things work themselves out the way that Jesus Himself did, in dirty barns, in darkness, on the run and completely unbecoming.

Turns out, in the unbecoming moments, we are becoming.

27 | BRIGHT SHINY NEW THINGS

◆

During the early months of 2012, Ryan and I began to dream of starting over. A real starting over. We knew it was time. It had been a year since Addison Road ended, we were on the heels of our ten-year wedding anniversary, which felt monumental, and within our incredibly tight-knit community group there was a sense that we were all about to head into vastly different directions. New jobs. New states. New babies. Personally we sensed our season of waiting was over and although we weren't exactly sure what came next, we knew it was time to make a move. A physical move. In May, we decided rather impulsively to move away from Texas for the first time in our married lives. We based the decision on the fact that our lease was coming to an end. Not exactly the booming divine voice that one might expect to guide such a decision. It was more like a holy hunch verses a divine decree.

And sometimes it is like that. Sometimes God doesn't tell us exactly where to go next or what to do when we get there; but He allows us the freedom to explore and boldly, bravely take a giant step into the direction we feel drawn. If you wait too long for God to part the heavens with a divine decree, you might forget that God has already given one:

choose life that you might live. Choose, He says. But I am often tempted to forgo the gifts of free will and choice because it seems easier to follow orders and mandates than to dream, to choose, to go. Our move to Nashville was based on a holy hunch, not a specific revelation. We made the choice to step into a divine mandate that had been given by God to His people a long, long time ago… we chose new life, that we might live.

I had been in Texas since I was nine years old and Ryan had never lived anywhere else. We needed a change of pace, a fresh start. A place that didn't look so much like the desert we had been living in, a place that physically represented the new life we were stepping into. We decided Nashville was a good fit. We already had friends living there, knew the names of most of the major highways, and knew how to get ourselves to and from the local Target. So really, what else can a woman ask for?

Our friends and family in Texas threw us a huge going away party. We sat around the pool in Texas, sipping wine and dangling our toes into the water with friends from childhood, sunday school teachers who had loved us well, along with our bandmates. And my heart suddenly ached. What are we doing? And why? And am I brave enough? Is it even necessary?

I was so ready to be out of the season of waiting, but leaving it felt more uncomfortable than I ever imagined it would. I kind of got good at the whole desert thing. It was all so second nature, living in the unknown of a broken life. Was I ready to be well? Was I whole enough to function like a normal person? And what if I got to the new place, the place on the other side of the in-between, and I hated it? Or it hated me? Could I make it in a non-deserty place, say, Boston? Would I even know how to be well?

Sometimes we are in the in-between for so long that we don't even know how to leave. We've lived without an exit strategy and leaving becomes harder than staying. The desert has become your friend; the waiting has become your home. Why venture out into a bright, shiny new place when I have become really good at the whole *living-in-the-dark-like-a-bat* thing?

For a brief moment, I was leery of new life the way I am leery of the mall kiosk lady who has a special array of lotions guaranteed to melt all of your thigh fat away. You want it to be true; you really do. But then it seems so far-fetched. And really, you've gotten used to your thighs. You even got a different wardrobe to work around those thighs. And you are comfortable where you are. Why risk it?

But I found myself at a going-away party, bidding farewell to an amazing community of friends, family, and memories and I was terrified to move out of the desert and into new life. Absolutely terrified. I didn't want to go away. I was really good at the desert.

My childhood friend Rebecca came and sat next to me, dangling her toes in the water. She had gone through her own journey of becoming and recently returned to Texas from a two-year stint in Colorado with her husband and sons. They, too, had left the only home they had ever known and ventured out into the great unknown. She too, knew the fear of jumping head long into new life. I waited for her to secretly whisper that it was okay to just stay put. It might be better. But what she said, in all its simplicity, opened wide the gate for new life in my heart.

"Jenny, you will be amazed at how giddy you get over the grocery store. Every day you will discover something new. The gas station. The local coffee shop. A park for Annie to play at. The neighborhood library. Everything will be new. Everything will be exciting. For the first year you will swear you have *never* been in a grocery store so good as the one you are in. You are going to LOVE it. I am so excited for you!"

It never occurred to me that what I was walking into was going to be an exciting adventure. That new life could be, well, *life-giving*. Bright, shiny, new things.

If finding bright shiny new things feels like it does when I clean out the back of my closet and discover the vintage coat I forgot I bought at Goodwill last season, I know it will feel good. If it's anything like finding an old letter from a friend in a shoebox, discovering twenty dollars in an unused purse or happening upon the perfect, hidden nook at the library…

anything like the first day of sixth grade with freshly sharpened, colored pencils

anything like the opening day of an Ikea…

anything like the first kiss that mattered…

anything like holding my newborn baby…

memorizing the way she sneezed and how her tiny breath felt against my chest…

if it feels anything like that, it's gonna feel good.

For the first time in years a window was cracked wide open inside of me and sun flooded the dusty corners of a heart that had learned to live well in the dark.

"When the time is right, the cocooned soul begins to emerge. Waiting turns golden. Newness unfurls. It's a time of pure, unmitigated wonder," Sue Monk Kidd says of the emerging season. Rebecca and Sue were both right, of course. We gawked at the mountains! (hills) that lined the horizon of Nashville like city walls. Annie marveled at the red and gold leaves while Ryan and I fumbled through our first fall; entranced by darkness that covered the city at 5:00 P.M. each chilly, November night. One morning we found ourselves at a Pumpkin farm! Not in the front lawn of a church or grocery store, the way we found pumpkins in Dallas, but on the back of a hay-covered tractor-trailer bringing us deep into the fields where thousands of orange balls grew wild. We lived in awe and wonder; it was a season of pumpkins and peace.

There will be a moment, you might well physically feel it, when someone will crack a window and you will startle. The light blinding your eyes. The fresh air strangely loose in your tight chest. The feel of the wind, not sand whipped and desert scorched, but Spring-made, sweet and dancing through your hair and across your face like a new breath from heaven. And it won't occur to you to be terrified. You will not decide to be brave or not. You will just be brave. You will welcome it. The sun and breeze and sweet smell of flowers. The light. You will put fingers on dusty windowsills and tears will course their way down your cheeks as the sun warms a face that has not seen pure light in far too long. And you will cry tears of joy. For the sun has come. It has finally come. And your heart will soar.

And that is how you know you are leaving the desert and happening upon new life.

Excitement begins to bubble at discovering the new thing that you were once terrified of. You are no longer grieving. No longer burying. No longer wallowing in the lostness, wondering if you will ever leave the desert. No longer wondering if there is another side and if you will ever get there.

You are on the other side, or very near there. There are glimmers of light, hope, promises, and new life.

You are on the outskirts of new. Giddy with small joys that until recently you never believed you would enjoy again. Even the spaghetti aisle feels full of potential.

Fear subsides and you feel brave. Today you will peek behind a bush. Turn over a rock. Eat a little more manna than you have previously rationed for yourself. Because, hey, it feels like you might be getting closer to civilization and that means a stockpile of manna. So today you rejoice and eat two pieces instead of one. You begin to live out of abundance again. Today you dream about the future in a way that you haven't. You open wide the possibility that you might be happy again. You might love again. You might have a house that doesn't burn to the ground. You might not be cursed after all! You are brave enough to dream about filling that house—that life—with things that matter. Dishes, a coffee pot, picture frames, friends. New friends that you will meet on the other side, in a place that brims with sunlight and shiny new things. Old friends, ones who always stood watch while you walked the in-between. You will bring them in, unafraid of the what-ifs.

There is no longer a possibility of new life.

There *is* new life. Coming in tiny moments of light, grace, laughter, and love.

Each day you will discover something new. And each day you will step a little more fully into newness. It's less like winning the lottery or stepping into a fortune fall of inheritance and more like recovering, a slow healing. I've yet to wake up and realize that I have walked into millions of dollars, but I've woken up to realize my limp is a little less. Each day is a few steps forward then a few steps back, but no longer lost in the desert. I'm headed somewhere new.

Soon, the burying, lostness, and waiting will be a fond memory of a place where you did really, really hard work with a gracious and faithful God. You will pick a day to remember it, to pay tribute to the long road traveled. But it will be, for this new season, only a remembrance; because now there is newness.

28 | THE CHORUS OF YOU CAN DO ITS

◆

I've become quite the bird watcher since moving from the concrete of North Texas to the lush rolling hills of middle Tennessee.

I live in a little row of condos that face a line of parking spots, a driveway, a chain link fence, and a row of privacy trees. Nothing fancy. But I'm convinced this row of privacy trees is where the most beautiful blue jays and red robins in the city have decided to call home. And I've never heard such a choir of birds in my life.

I've also never had a front porch that faces east, or a front porch for that matter. I've never woken up in Texas and gone outside in the middle of the summer to find a cool breeze greeting me with hellos. Nashville might as well be Northern Michigan. Every day, I go to my front porch to watch the sun rise and feel the crisp breeze and be with my birds.

I wish I could put an ID system together so I could tell the birds apart, because I have theories. Watch birds long enough and you'll have your own theories.

The birds like my front yard the best. I think this is because we don't keep up with proper lawn care, so we have a premium selection of worms lurking beneath our deep sea of grass. The birds come to our tiny sliver of yard each morning and they get their food the same way each time.

They hop twice. Then they look down and bob their heads twice, not yet touching the earth. Then, they turn twenty-five degrees to their right and in one fatal swoop, they bob their heads down into the muddy earth and come back up with a long, wriggly, muddy worm. Then they fly away and eat it in the tree. It's like clockwork. Every time it's double hop, double bob, twenty-five degree turn, and worm victory.

Today, the baby birds were given the boot and forced to come look for worms alone. That's my theory. They are little and cute and perky. And they are lost. They are actually quite terrible at procuring food. They are not nearly as efficient as their elders. They do three hops instead of two, and way too many head bobs to keep track of. Some of them look frozen. Like they need someone to give them a little nudge and remind them to keep breathing.

They are making too much noise to be effective. They are talking to each other and they aren't supposed to be. And I know their mommas are in the trees watching them and giving them guidance, but I just kind of have the urge to chime in too.

Baby Birds! Shhhhh. You are giving the worms way too much warning.

Shhhhh. You have to surprise them like your mommas do.

I lean in. As if the birds understand human-pajama-girl language. I whisper.

That's it! Tiptoe! You're doing it sweet little bird!

Now, ATTACK! ATTACK! BOB YOUR HEAD. BE RUTHLESS.

I sigh and shake my head.

It's okay. We can try again tomorrow. You will get one.

They fly back to their trees with empty beaks. And I feel sad for them. Disappointed for their failure. A few minutes later, the baby birds fly back down and try all over again. And fail all over again. I feel sad for them all over again. The cycle repeats itself several times as I sit on the porch, trying to read. Trying to pray.

Somewhere along the way, in the middle of feeling sad for the baby birds, I realize that the choir of birds chirping and whistling is louder than normal. And it's constant. Beautiful songs, echoing relentlessly as the baby birds come and totally botch their assignment to find worms.

Sure, they are failing, but they are doing so in the midst of a sea of beautiful voices. And I like to think those voices are their mommas and daddies, bird cousins and pigeon friends, cheering them on with *You Can DO Its* as they fail miserably at their first attempts to search for sustenance.

I am such a creepy bird lady now, audibly cheering on baby birds in my front yard.

And I am crying happy tears because I theorize that their families are cheering them on too.

Oh, the gift of the chorus that cheers us on with *You Can Do Its* when we are out by ourselves, searching for life. Searching for promised lands. Searching for what lies deep beneath the surface, unseen to the naked eye. Searching. Wandering.

Sometimes it's family and friends. Other times it's the strange bird-lady on the outside, wholly unrelated to you and unaware of any of your story, except the part that matters the most, the moment at hand. And they are keeping the nest together; keeping the lifelines afloat. The person from the outside willing to cheer you on as you go searching. And the ones from within, willing to watch you crash and burn a few times and come back to the nest empty-handed, and still sing out to you:

we believe in you

you will figure it out

and when you bring back your first worm

we are gonna have a *huge* party

And the truth is, sometimes I don't want the chorus there cheering me on. I don't want a group of cheerleaders to come cheer me on as I come up empty-handed. Uncertain of what my next move will be, uncertain if I can keep trying, uncertain if I have what it takes to find life, uncertain if I was ever good enough to be a bird in the first place. I don't want people to see me fail.

There are so many moments, I just want them to all go away. Them, with their put-together lives and hefty checking accounts and dreams already come true. Just go away with your encouragement already. I am flailing out here. Digging for worms in the mud. Just let me do it in pathetic privacy please, because maybe I wasn't cut out for this whole thing. Maybe I should just go back home. And I don't want you to see me turn around and walk the other way, back to the nest, empty-handed.

But that chorus who stands in unity, piping their voices out over me knows something that I don't.

Solo flights, while ultimately walked alone, are never successful without a choir of voices watching from the rafters, whispering and yelling YOU CAN DO IT, holding their breath and waiting in angst with you as you slowly, painfully, and broken make your way to the other side.

And that's why the chorus is in it for the long haul. The choir of voices saying *you can do it.*

It's hard to turn around and walk back to where you came from when there is a choir cheering you on to new life. It's the ultimate walk of shame. But when they are there watching, holding their breath, nudging you on, waiting, waiting, waiting with you. Knowing there is another side. Believing you will reach it. Believing for you when you can't. Watching with graceful eyes as you flail about, because they too have fallen, flailed and found new life on the other side. When they are there refusing to let you be invisible. Refusing to relegate themselves to the before and after, the easiest parts of the story. Refusing to do anything but sing over you as you bob around looking for worms. You slowly adopt their rhythms and mantras of grace and faith. You believe, because they have believed over you. Perhaps, you might just make it after all. The choir of voices sings over you a song so rich in faith and perseverance and presence that you get the feeling they might be in it for the long haul. They might just sing over you the entire time you are wandering. Wandering. Wandering.

Where would I be without my choir?

My mom, Jackie, Krista, Missy, Aubrey, Becca, Lauren, Amy, Betsy, Melissa, Sarah, Kristen, Claire?

How would I make it?

I wouldn't.

So I sit on my front porch, morning after morning, unashamed to be the other voice calling out to the birds, telling them they can do it! And they remind me why it's important to let a choir of people sing over me while I flounder too. And honestly, it's uncomfortable for everyone involved. Me talking to birds, and friends singing and cheering me on while I crash and burn and hangout in lonely, barren wilderness for long stretches of time. It's uncomfortable. But getting into someone's story, being committed to wait and wait and wait and cheer them on with whispers and prayers and screams while they make their way flying solo, crossing from weariness to wilderness to water holes to promised lands always is.

Give me the choir. I want them singing behind me, even the creepy bird lady. Without the choir, it's way too easy to turn around and go back to where I came from. Or set up camp in the in-between. But my choir says no. They cheer me on. They annoy me with their constant presence. They wait in the shadows with faith more sturdy than mine. And they sing their songs, balms of grace, over my journey.

And sometimes, for me, the choir needs to know a reeeeaaaallly long song and come prepared with a few cases of water. But that's okay. Good choirs are ready for that. Maybe that's why Handel wrote *Messiah*. It's just long enough for a choir to sing over someone trying to find their way out of the wilderness. Trying to find worms. Taking baby steps into new life.

Let the choir sing over you. Don't turn their voices away. Let them sing.

Let their *He Shall Reigns* carry you.

29 | SHOVELS, PRISON, AND OTHER HEAVENLY THINGS

◆

My mom called recently with the sound of a bleating goat in the background. I immediately knew this was a problem since my mom doesn't own a goat or live near a goat and there is no reason she should have possession of a goat. The goat was bleating at the top of its lungs. It sounded like she might be dying or having a baby goat. It sounded like the goat was on top of my mom, who was hollering into the phone, "She won't stop! She won't stop!" All I could envision was the eulogy I would have to give for my mom and how angry I would be if she died because she was attacked by a goat.

We've warned her about these things. My sisters and I have told her, "We will NOT come to your funeral if you get killed by one of your pet animals, Mom. We are serious, Mom. Mom, are you listening? MOM!" We throw around the word "mom" a lot in those conversations to remind her that she is, in fact, our mother and has a God-given obligation to be there for us when we need to cry, cuss, and crash. We like to remind her she is bound to us, till death do us part. And that death by goat, or any other pet, is not acceptable.

My mom doesn't actually have any pets in the house, but she lives in the country and no animal is a stranger to her. They are all her friends. She has named them. She leaves out cat food and a bowl of milk for the family of raccoons that comes to the back porch each night. She talks to the horses like they know and understand every word she speaks. And when my parents owned a family of longhorn, she could often be found petting them and singing children's songs or Neil Diamond to them.

Sarah especially despises how carelessly my mom befriends animals with horns, rabies, and sharp teeth. Sarah is the youngest in the family and doesn't like change. She is a big fan of tradition, well laid plans and Christmas schedules that ensure everyone is in the same house on the same morning. She has protested every family move or major change in tradition since the moment she entered our world. She is our little activist, you might say. And the day my mom and dad keel over is not going to be an easy one for her. She is a BIG fan of not rushing that day. So Mom really throws a lot of kinks into Sarah's plans of safety and longevity for our family. That probably explains why I got the first phone call when mom confiscated a live farm animal.

My mom is a preacher and that particular morning the sermon was about sheep. So she rented a goat from a neighbor down the street to use as an example. *Because that is what normal pastors do.* They rent a goat from the next door neighbor, put it loose in the car for a thirty-minute drive, sing to it in an effort to calm it down, call her daughter to bemoan the fact that the goat is not responding to the singing of *Jesus Loves Me*, and bring it unannounced, into a pristine, one-hundred-year-old sanctuary.

She called one time on another Sunday morning to tell me she had locked her keys in the house and couldn't get into her car to drive to church. I told her to call a locksmith. She responded that they don't work on Sundays. This is blatantly untrue. They make a lot of money to work on Sundays, I tell her. She texted me back minutes later, "You're *never* going to believe this! I found a shovel sitting behind the garage! I didn't even know we owned a shovel! I'm just going to use that."

Dad was temporarily living a thousand miles away and couldn't stop her. But I knew he would not approve. I try to intervene and talk her off the ledge, but it's too late. The damage has already been done. She texts back several minutes later to let me know she has smashed in the back door of the house with a shovel and is leaving the house wide open, with glass strewn about, and driving to church so she can preach her sermon. A pastor has to do what a pastor has to do. She hopes the raccoons don't come in the house while she is away. Oh, and she never liked that back door anyway.

My dad lives a thousand miles away from my mom because he is in the military. *Still* in the military. And this is nothing short of a miracle. My dad, the kid from small-town Mississippi, who joined the service as soon as he turned eighteen and went to boot camp as soon as he graduated high school is now a General, working at one of the highest levels in the Air National Guard. A man who was never active duty and did not deploy to the front lines of a major war, leads Chaplains all over the country. It's his dream job. My sisters and I are his biggest fans. My mom is his cheerleader. This was never how it was supposed to happen for Dad. We all knew that. This was way out of his league. At least twenty years ago it was. We remember those days. Those days when we watched Dad and learned that sometimes dreams crash and burn.

But these days we watch Dad and learn that sometimes dreams run big and deep and wide and new dreams spring up. Different dreams. Bigger dreams. Dreams so big we never knew to dream them on our own. Dreams so big that we are not brave enough or vain enough or crazy enough to allow ourselves to think we might be at the end of such lofty heights. Dreams so audacious, they are divine.

I believe divine things happen all the time because I believe God still shows up. Sometimes through a job that you never had the vision to dream. A check in the mail, groceries on the doorstep, or turning the radio on to the perfect song at the perfect moment. Divine moments come through a whisper, reminding me of who I am and how deeply I am loved and treasured. They come through a gentle breeze, a sunset, the finding of a long lost friend or the sudden memory of where you left the keys when you really need to get in the car and drive. And yes, sometimes, divine moments come through a shovel when you need to smash the back door in. Where there is life, the Divine is alive and at work.

The divine presence of God is making Himself known at all times, often in the most peculiar, unexpected places.

One time I saw God show up at a prison. A few years back, I was performing a Christmas concert in a federal women's prison. I was scared to death. It was not my finest moment. Most of the morning was spent in prayer for a prison riot or kitchen fire to break out so I would, unfortunately, not be able to go through with the show. I practiced my look of disappointment, sure that I would be rescued from the perils of performing for mean, criminal ladies who were going to hate me and murder me with their eye-ball stares. Deep down the fear was that I had nothing to offer them. That we were so different from one another they would certainly write me off as a privileged girl from the suburbs who hadn't lived a real life.

Walking in, knowing I had nothing to offer, I began to sweat profusely. Still, like a stubborn child, I begged for an escape. Instead of preparing my heart to love and share and give, I prayed selfish prayers. "For the love of all that's holy, deliver me, JESUS! I will go to Africa! I will go to nursing homes! Anywhere but here!" With my back to the women walking in, I stood in a panic, begging for the exit. And that's when I heard a quiet whisper from Jesus. I'm not sure of the exact words, or if there even were words, just a sense to turn around and look at the girls. A sense that God was with me and asking me to trust Him and reminding me that indeed, these women were God's daughters.

I turned around in fear. Knot in my throat, trembling and sweating. And that's when I heard the most beautiful words of my entire life.

"Oh my gosh, JENNY? *YOU ARE* Addison Road?!?"

The first prisoner I laid eyes on was a long-lost friend from junior high and high school.

A thousand miles away from home, ten years after our high school graduation, in a prison in Greenville, Illinois, I came face to face with a friend I had grown up with and loved dearly. We even volunteered together, taking care of the special ed students at our high school on a weekly basis.

Tears streamed down her face as she laughed and smiled and cried. And the women around her? Tears ran down their faces too. They all knew Randi loved Jesus. They all knew Randi had been desperately lonely, praying and fasting for a taste of home. They all knew that it was the week before Christmas and this was a divine gift; an answer to Randi and her family's prayers. As I ran to Randi and broke all the rules and picked her up and hugged her—even the male guards had tears running down their cheeks.

The next two hours we sang like sisters. The whole room full of convicts and me sang like long lost sisters. *Silent Night* and *Jingle Bells* and *Holy is the Lord* and *Hope Now* and even some Bruno Mars tunes. We sang them at the top of our lungs. And Randi wiped away tears and I wiped away tears. The girl mixed up in dealing drugs and the girl begging God for prison riots. Childhood friends from a thousand miles away, in the same prison the week before Christmas. I stood in amazement of the Divine at work.

When I know I have nothing left to offer and have perhaps just put my absolute worst foot forward, that is when I suspect God might show up. His strength in my weakness serves as a reminder to the world around me that through broken people—beauty and healing come. The Divine comes. And the becoming—that place of newness and wholeness—arrives.

In every divine moment I am reminded of the words of Julian of Norwich all over again. "But all shall be well and all shall be well and all manner of thing shall be well." Not because of the broken person, the one praying for prison riots and such. But because of the God who is behind them and in them and through them. The God who is ever at work, divinely making all things well.

What do I know of holy? I thought I knew a lot when I was younger. I had faith that believed in angels, demons, miracles, and visions. It was not the faith of a particular denomination or a teacher; it was the kind of faith I knew instinctively as a small child. Faith made possible by innocence and my ability to see with a different set of eyes. Madeleine L'Engle says we cannot lose those eyes, "The artist, if he is not to forget how to listen, must retain the vision which includes angels and dragons and unicorns and all the lovely creatures which our world would put in a box marked *Children Only*." But sometimes I am afraid I might be losing my eyesight.

The older I have gotten, the more like Nicodemus I am tempted to become.

Jesus says to him, "Don't be surprised when I say, 'You must be born again.' The wind blows wherever it wants. Just as you can hear the wind but can't tell where it comes from or where it is going, so you can't explain how people are born of the Spirit."

"How are these things possible?" Nicodemus asked.

Jesus replied, "You are a respected Jewish teacher, and yet you don't understand these things? I assure you, we tell you what we know and have seen, and yet you won't believe our testimony. But if you don't believe me when I tell you about earthly things, how can you possibly believe if I tell you about heavenly things?"

The offer stands. Jesus says to Nicodemus that if he could only believe, He would tell Nicodemus heavenly things. Jesus says to me if I will only believe, He will tell *me* heavenly things. Earthly things and heavenly things and God things seem hard to grasp some days. And yet the person who has finally stepped out of the in-between seasons of burying, lostness, and waiting, and into the brand new life of becoming has learned a thing or two about living with eyes that have not lost the ability to see the Divine at work. They know the Divine is always, ever at work. And they are unmistakably in the middle of it all.

30 | SAYING YES

◆

This is how I say yes to the life at hand.

I wake up each morning and I go downstairs. I open the blinds and watch the sun stream into my living room window as it rises in the east. This is a pre-requisite for living. Windows that face east and west. Sunrises and sunsets.

I brew my first cup of coffee and crack the windows. I like to listen to the birds as they wake up the world.

I go to the front porch. I breathe deep. And all this in a house that doesn't belong to me. In a rental condo! Imagine that! I have come to terms with it. So I'm not a homeowner and I have a bad credit score because of one year in my life that beat us up and spit us out financially. A theft, car accident, daughter's surgery, and ravaging fire will do that. Who cares? I just don't anymore. I have a front porch and windows facing east and west. My daughter sleeps in a room she loves. And the walls of the place we call home right now are a testament to a life lived deep and wide. A life of dreams, detours, and rebirth that created a life worth living and a story worth telling. Does anything else truly matter?

I don't look at the empty spots on the calendar with negativity where tour schedules used to dominate. I look at empty spots on the calendar and smile. Shall Annie and I play in the leaves or paint? Will I write a story, a blog, or a card to my grandma? Will I sing to a room of high school girls or teach a songwriting class? I'm no longer interested in what was; I am only interested in what will become. Of course there are moments when a voice tries to creep in and remind me of long-gone dreams and plans and tries to bid me come and feel sorry for myself. Some days I do. I cry and pout and walk around in a firestorm of anger. I call it re-grieving. And re-grieving is *totally* acceptable. But I am learning that these moments of re-grief are less and less about the actual dreams I buried and more about the current place I find myself in. The current place that longs for my days to count. Longs for a life rich in friends, family, faith, and fearlessness. It's when I feel my current days are coming up short that I am most tempted to believe that my buried dreams would have delivered the life results I wanted. Sure, there are tiny moments I grieve what was, but more than that, I am aching for meaning now.

These days I remember that the answer is not behind me; it is in front of me. It is in this very moment. And God seems to constantly be inviting me to say yes to the life in front of me. The words of God to the Israelites in Deuteronomy 30 are on a constant reel in my mind.

Now what I am commanding you today is not too difficult for you or beyond your reach. It is not up in heaven, so that you have to ask, "Who will ascend into heaven to get it and proclaim it to us so we may obey it?" Not is it beyond the sea, so that you have to ask, "Who will cross the sea to get it and proclaim it to us so we may obey it?" No, the word is very near you; it is in your mouth and in your heart so you may obey it. See, I set before you today life and prosperity, death and destruction... Now choose life that you and your children may live.

God's daily invitation to choose life is always before me prodding me to say yes to the moment at hand. So I live simply and with purpose. How can I love my next-door neighbor well today? This is hard because she has five dogs that bark all the time and I hate barking dogs. But I am learning to say yes to even her place in my life. I say yes to making space, making lunches, making new friends, making a solo album that my record label is confident will make a big impact. I call the album *The Becoming*. I pour my heart and soul into it. Songs for people burying, being lost, waiting, and becoming new. Songs to remind people that God shows up on this road to becoming. It releases in the spring of 2013 and doesn't sell a hundred thousand copies or top any type of radio charts. In fact, radio won't play the songs at all, there are no tour offers, and I barely sell 5,000 albums. I've sold more boxes of Girl Scout cookies than this. The people who once partnered with me in the music industry decide that they can't partner with me anymore because I can't sell enough units; I'm not commercially successful enough for them. My record label and publishing house of eight years drops me.

But I still say yes. This is not failure, this is living. And I have lived long enough to know that dreams, goals, partnerships, people, plans and passions come and go. Change is constant and learning to live with open hands is the best gift I can give myself, my family and my God. Saying yes to the moment at hand is my only commodity.

So in this new season, I have an album of songs I believe in. I created it out of nothing—what a gift. Who cares if there is no record label, radio play or commercial success? I say yes to faithfully championing these songs of holy becoming, whether I'm lucrative to anyone else or not. The songs are true and honest and inspired. They are my offering to the Lord and I will keep giving that offering away no matter what. New life looks a lot like saying yes to the opportunities and people right in front of my nose.

I make a healthy dinner. I learn to cook and even iron! I write stories and tell stories from small stages. My only focus is choosing life each new day, not a ten-year map to hustle and success. I am faithful to the little things.

Mark Buchanan describes my life as of late in his transformative book, *The Rest of God.* "I used to think the spiritual life was mostly about finding and using our gifts for God's glory- my utmost for his highest. More and more, I think it is not this, not first, not most. At root, the spiritual life consists in choosing the way of littleness."

Toward the end of my time in Addison Road, I remember sipping coffee and talking with a wildly respected lady who walks with artists in their personal and artistic lives. I told her how tired I was. Depleted and empty. She asked me if God needed me to be a martyr, to work myself in the ground with travel and music and making art. And I will never forget what came next. "Would God be just as pleased if you moved into a little cottage on a lake somewhere and spent your days listening to birds, praising God for His creation, and attending to your husband, daughter, and your own soul?"

I was appalled. Of *course* God would mind. I had a gift, a calling! My utmost for His highest was in high demand! The idea of living little seemed wasteful; it wasn't part of the dream.

Thinking back to that conversation, I know the groundwork was being laid for where I am now. As if she meant to say, "One day you will choose what is best for you. You will choose life that you may live. And that may mean saying yes to a different type of road. A new type of dream."

On the road to becoming I realized that the dream, with its grandiose happily-ever-after, only lasts for a brief moment. Dreams are hard earned, short-lived, and always leave us wanting more. Mountaintops are a small part of our journeys; they are not the whole of our existence or the only moments that matter in a life. Annie Dillard sums up mountain top moments better than anyone, "I have never understood why so many mystics of all creeds experience the presence of God on mountaintops. Aren't they afraid of being blown away?" Truth is, we look for God on mountaintops when God might be just as pleased to meet us at a cottage by the lake.

Saying yes and choosing life doesn't look the same in every season. Sometimes it absolutely happens on a mountaintop. But most of our moments, this side of heaven, unfold in valleys, deserts, minivans, long commutes, quiet cottages by the lake, around the table and on flat land—-rich with friendship and fertile soil. We shed skin, lie dormant, and regenerate as all living, breathing things must do. This isn't high altitude living.

I love my husband and I love my daughter. I try to make their lives more rich and beautiful. I go to parks and take pictures of Annie's newest creations. I cook dinner. Well, I try to cook dinner. I still haven't gotten used to the fact that people cook Every. Single. Day. I check in on my sisters and my family. I nurture friendships. I write the stories of beauty and redemption that I see unfolding around me. I play.

These days I am faithful to little things. The end of my movie? It's not a cinematic masterpiece, the make-believe kind that you watch on the big screens. But I know now that it was never supposed to be. The lady who walks with artists knew what I didn't. She knew that gifts and callings change shape; and some seasons are best spent tending to the cottage so the soul can be renewed and restored. Living in the way of littleness, a way that doesn't demand my martyrdom, is how I say yes to Jesus these days.

So what of the dream? The one conjured up all those years ago in the magnolia tree, when all of life was attentive to my whim and whimsy?

Maybe the dream comes to fruition or perhaps it crashes and burns. Maybe a new dream springs up. One so deep and wide and beyond my wildest expectations that I have won the proverbial lottery of dreams. Or maybe I find myself somewhere in between.

It doesn't matter.

The end of the story isn't dependent on the state of the dream.

The end of the story isn't about answers and prosperity and happily-ever-afters.

The end of the story is about something more rich and beautiful and constant than dreams, which are here today and gone tomorrow. The end of the story is about living *whatever the story is* well.

I think it looks a little more like being brave enough to take one step after the other. To keep going. To keep becoming. To allow the cycle to play out. To refuse to bury my head in the sand and ignore reality. To refuse to cling to the past, turning down my much-needed burial rights. My life is more about stepping into the lostness than stepping into happily-ever-after. Knowing and trusting that in the lost and waiting, new life is being uncovered and stumbled upon. I am becoming. And I am not alone. In a mysterious way that I will never understand, God is with me.

The end of the story looks less like an earth-answer and more like Jesus. Jesus doesn't say, "Come to me, all ye who are weary and I will give you an answer." He says, "Come to me, all ye who are weary and I will give you rest." We have not been called to answers. We have been called to Jesus. And it's maddening really. When Jesus was asked questions by the religious people, who so desperately wanted Jesus to lay out black and white answers, He would often answer by asking more questions.

Who are you, Jesus?

Who do you say I am?

Teacher, what must I do to inherit eternal life?

What is written in the law? How do you read it?

Who is my neighbor?

Which of these do you think was a neighbor to the man?

We crave clear-cut answers, but God insists on relationship. God asks us questions because, Mark Buchanan says, "Nothing hooks us and pries us open quite like a question. You can talk all day at me, yet it obliges me nothing. I can listen or not, respond or not. But ask me one question, and I must answer or rupture our fellowship. God's inquisitiveness, His seeming curiosity, is a measure of His intimate nature. He desires relationship."

Sometimes it's more questions than answers. An empty canvas is hard for the over-worked, over-stimulated, over-committed person to accept. Cottages and the way of littleness? No thanks. But could it be, when Jesus says to pick up our cross and follow Him, He means to follow Him into the backwardness of it all? Detours, unbecoming moments, mapless ways through wastelands. Life abundant coming from the least likely places—is this what it means to follow Jesus? Journeying down our road to becoming with full faith that burying, lostness, and waiting are gateways to new life.

These days I get the feeling that the way of the cross is less concerned with answers and more concerned with Jesus. Not Plan A, Plan B, Plan

F. Not happily-ever-after. Not even concrete answers. Just an empty canvas, a new day, and saying yes to the holy unknown. Saying yes to new life, unexpected joys, and unknown roads. These days I don't have a five-year plan or even a five-month plan. There is no map and I live with open hands. The heartbeat and prayer that guides our family now is alarmingly simple.

We wake up each new day and say yes.

Yes, to being a part of God's story.

Chances are I will make a wrong turn or two, or twenty. The world may throw a kink into my plan. The world *will* throw a kink into my plan. Detours are inevitable. A friend, child, or closest family member might hurt me; their decision crippling my dream. I might grow ill or lose all my earthly possessions. Odds are, at some point you and I will end up broken and lost on the side of a road less traveled. But even in this, I have learned to reshape my questions. Instead of being consumed with *Why did the road end? Why me? What now?* I am learning to ask, *Am I traveling this road well? Leaning into each season, opening my hands, falling into trust, waiting as God grows new things inside of me?* Because those are the things that really matter.

I don't need a map anymore, which is good, because the road to becoming is mapless. All I need is a guide who knows the way to the other side. No matter how many times the road changes. How many times it veers and turns, switches and cuts back. If I am still in the middle of this unknown, messy, redemptive journey alongside Jesus then my becoming is bearable—beautiful, even.

With every unexpected detour, my prayer is this: May new life begin to take root and grow, even now, as I bury the road behind me, sit blindly in my lostness and wait for holy hunches. May I reach the end of this detour in awe and wonder; marveling at blossoms that have pushed through earth and soil to become. And may God send spaghetti angels, choirs singing their He Shall Reign, shovels and Cracker Barrel rescues all along the way.

Because I am a part of God's story, no matter what road I find myself on,

it is well
and all shall be well
and all manner of thing shall be well.

NOTES

CHAPTER 2: **A Beginner's Dream**

1. Glennon Melton, *Carry On, Warrior: Thoughts on Life Unarmed* (New York: Scribner, 2013), 7.

CHAPTER 4: **Epiphanies**

1. Madeleine L'Engle, *Walking on Water: Reflections on Faith and Art* (Colorado Springs, CO: Shaw, 2001), 26.

CHAPTER 6: **A Bad Year**

1. Judith Viorst, *Alexander and the Terrible, Horrible, No Good, Very Bad Day* (New York: Atheneum, 1987).

CHAPTER 9: **Ants and Other Holy Thoughts**

1. Dr. Jackie Roese and Steve Roese were our pastors, friends, therapists and the driving force behind our family-dinner-get-togethers during the season that the stories in this book were lived out. Steve and Jackie left an indelible mark on our faith and family; they brought us to Jesus time and time again. This book would not exist, in this form, had it not been for their tireless love, friendship and commitment to the gritty, uncomfortable, gloriously redemptive story of Jesus that they offered so freely around their kitchen table. They continue to boldly, beautifully shape the world around them through their individual ministries, The Marcella Project and Water is Basic. **www.marcellaproject.com | www.waterisbasic.com**

CHAPTER 11: **Aisle 7 and Evil Spaghetti**

1. Jesus grieves the death of John the Baptist in Matthew 14:13-36.

CHAPTER 12: **Dead Goldfish and a Holy Summons**

1. Walter Isaacson, *Benjamin Franklin: An American Life* (New York: Simon & Schuster, 2003), 258.
2. "Goodbye Mr. Fish." *The Cosby Show.* NBC. 27 Sept. 1984. Television.

CHAPTER 13: **Poor Rich Man**

1. Mark 10 paraphrased.
2. The story of Elijah and the widow of Zarephath can be found in 1 Kings 17:7-16.

CHAPTER 15: **Iowa Cornfield**

1. Isaiah 45:3, New Revised Standard Version.

CHAPTER 16: **Lost Girl**

1. Robert Benson, *The Echo Within: Finding Your True calling* (Colorado Springs, CO: WaterBrook, 2009), 57.
2. Ecclesiastes 3:6, New Living Translation.
3. Wendell Berry, *Standing By Words: Essays* (Berkeley, CA: Counterpoint, 2011).

CHAPTER 18: **Joshua Tree**

1. Jesus promised the Great Comforter in John 14:16 and 16:1-7.
2. Henri Nouwen, *The Return of the Prodigal Son: A Story of Homecoming* (New York: Image, 1994), 40.
3. Job 33 paraphrased.
4. Isaiah 43: 18-21, New International Version.

CHAPTER 19: **Beauty in the Desert**

1. Jonathan Martin, *Prototype: What Happens When You Discover You're More Like Jesus Than You Think?* (Carol Stream, IL: Tyndale Momentum, 2013), 26.
2. Psalm 23 paraphrased.
3. Henri Nouwen, *The Return of the Prodigal Son: A Story of Homecoming* (New York: Image, 1994), 35.
4. Jonathan Martin, *Prototype: What Happens When You Discover You're More Like Jesus Than You Think?* (Carol Stream, IL: Tyndale Momentum, 2013), 50.

CHAPTER 20: **Motel 6**

1. Mark Buchanan, *The Rest of God: Restoring Your Soul by restoring Sabbath* (Nashville: W Publishing Group, 2006), 84.
2. Psalm 139, The Voice Translation.
3. Sue Monk Kidd, *When The Heart Waits: Spiritual Direction for Life's Sacred Questions* (San Francisco: HarperCollins, 1990), 88.

CHAPTER 21: **The River**

1. Nicole Nordeman, *"Rolling River God," Wide Eyed* (Sparrow Records: 1998).
2. Foster, Richard. Forward. *Embracing the Love of God: The Path and Promise of Christian Life.* By James Bryan Smith. New York: Harper Collins, 1995. xiv. Print.
3. Shauna Niequist, *Bread and Wine: A Love Letter to Life Around the Table, With Recipes* (Grand Rapids, Michigan: Zondervan, 2013), 59.

CHAPTER 23: **The Spiritual Director Doctor**

1. My time with Dr. Troy Caldwell was short in days, but long in impact. Troy has written profoundly about the human soul and spiritual direction in his book, *Adventures in Soulmaking: Discovering the Kingdom Within.* His website is a well-stocked treasury for those seeking further guidance in the way of contemplation and spiritual direction. **www.troycaldwell.com**

CHAPTER 24: **Fat Feet and Waiting Games**

1. Sue Monk Kidd, *When The Heart Waits: Spiritual Direction for Life's Sacred Questions* (San Francisco: HarperCollins, 1990), 14.
2. Quote attributed to A.W. Tozer; source unknown.

CHAPTER 25: **Growing Something New**

1. Frederick Schmidt, *What God Wants for Your Life: Finding Answers to the Deepest Questions* (San Francisco: HarperCollins, 2005), 200.

CHAPTER 26: **Overrated**

1. Jennie Allen, *Anything: The Prayer that Unlocked My God and My Soul* (Nashville: Thomas Nelson, 2011).
2. Barbara Robinson, *The Best Christmas Pageant Ever* (New York: Harper Trophy, 2005), 67.

CHAPTER 27: **Bright Shiny New Things**

1. Deuteronomy 30:19
2. Sue Monk Kidd, *When The Heart Waits: Spiritual Direction for Life's Sacred Questions* (San Francisco: HarperCollins, 1990), 177.

CHAPTER 29: **Shovels, Prison and Other Heavenly Things**

1. Julian of Norwich, *Revelations of Divine Love* (Public Domain) Thirteenth Revelation, chapter XXVII.
2. Madeleine L'Engle, *Walking on Water: Reflections on Faith and Art* (Colorado Springs, CO: Shaw, 2001), 14.
3. The story of Nicodemus can be found in John 3.

CHAPTER 30: **Saying Yes**

1. Mark Buchanan, *The Rest of God: Restoring Your Soul by restoring Sabbath* (Nashville: W Publishing Group, 2006), 101.
2. Annie Dillard, *The Annie Dillard Reader* (New York: Harper Collins, 1995), 334.
3. Mark Buchanan, *The Rest of God: Restoring Your Soul by restoring Sabbath* (Nashville: W Publishing Group, 2006), 209-210.

ACKNOWLEDGEMENTS

It takes a village to raise a child—and a book. The beautifully redemptive ending to this story was made possible by those who journeyed alongside me during the long days of my becoming. So many people met Ryan and I in the midst of our broken dreams and offered us hope; so many people brought us to Jesus. This is my attempt at thanking them.

To my parents, Steve and Debbie Chisolm: For your unrelenting, blind and merciful love and generosity that seems to know no bounds in my life. This story was made possible because a long time ago you followed a God-sized epiphany and you taught us to do the same. When the dreams fell apart, you taught us how to move forward and reminded us why moving forward mattered. That you have been in church ministry our entire lives and Melissa, Sarah and I still love Jesus and believe the Church is good, is a testament to you both. Thank you for giving us the freedom to dream, explore, chase, fail, come back home, repeat. This book is as much yours as it is mine. Thank you for letting me share our family's story. I love you more than words can say.

To my sisters, Melissa and Sarah: I cannot imagine my life without you. You love fiercely and beautifully. My story- this story- cannot be told without your profound presence touching it. I may be the oldest but you girls have lived through life's most unspeakable pains and done so with a beauty, grace, perseverance and strength that I can only dream of having. Thank you for letting me share our family's story. I love you more than words can say.

To my in-laws, Howell and Ila: Your love and prayers have covered us for well over a million miles on the ground and in the air. Your faithfulness to your church, your sons and your on-the-road grandparent-duties has been a constant, beautiful reminder of the sacrificial love of God. Our story is different because you believed in our ministry and our calling when we didn't have the courage or strength to believe in it ourselves. We love you more than words could say.

To my bandmates, Ryan Gregg, Travis Lawrence, and Jeff Sutton: If I could do it all over again, I wouldn't choose anyone else to spend ten years with. Who would have ever thought that the songs we created would bring hope to people around the world? I could not be more proud of what we created together. For every laugh, tear, venue, state, band-fight, podcast, fire, theft, ice-storm, hail-storm, tornado and hurricane we lived through together… I am immeasurably more rich. You are the best men I know and I love you.

To our sunday-night-family-dinner group: Jackie, Steve, Gregg, Krista, Amy, Betsy, Aubrey, Joey, Laurie, John, Bear, Becca, Joy, Madison and Kelly. We walked through HELL together. Y'all remember that? All of us, all at once. How incredibly kind of the Lord to give us one another for that season. You journeyed with Ryan and I in the most raw, painful, financially ruined, broken spaces and you nursed us back to life (whether we wanted it or not!). Those nights around the kitchen table changed the course of our lives. This book bears witness to light, not darkness, because of your presence. What an amazing forever-family we have.

To long-time friends: Sam Smith, Alvin and Debbie Wade, Jason and Christy Gadman, Todd and Vonda Hellner, Mike and Patti Work, Kim and Leon Verriere, Scott Hoffmeyer, Rebecca Wells, Brandi Wells, Megan Claunch, Elizabeth Davis, Erik Milam and Lani and Jarod Hofacket. Your love, support and insane belief in us over the years has carried us more times than we can count. We have often continued down our road to becoming because of your presence in our lives. We love you and are so grateful for you.

To my girl-friends new and old: Without you I just COULD. NOT. DO. IT. For every plate of Mexican food, cupcake, laugh, cry, prayer or late night lightning storm- thank you. Lauren Patterson, Missy McElroy, Kristen Maher, Claire St. Amant, Kara Gillum, Lindsay Nobles, Jackie Brewster, Franny Goodwin, Jamie Jamgochian, Lindsay McCaul, Jodi King, Emily Moffit, Karen Briseno, Kara Zapata, Morgan Fite and Jessie Reisman.

To the amazing team of ladies who handled this book with keen eyes, open minds and big hearts: Jana Burson (editor) Anna Floit (copy-editor) Lindsay Hartz (project manager) and Emily Lambright (interior design). I am incredibly honored to work with talent and heart like yours. Well done.

To my managers: Andy Goerlich, Tony Potato and the entire FUEL management team. WE DID IT. You have championed me from day one and I could NOT do this without you. Thank you for working tirelessly, with passion, excellence and always thinking outside the box. I'm glad we are a team.

And finally to the 464 Kickstarter backers who believed in this book before they ever read a single word: You gave me the rare gift of making this dream a reality and I cannot thank you enough for joining me in this dream-making. May you find grace, hope and companionship as you journey down your own road to becoming. This book is for you. Special thanks to Kickstarter backers:

Scott and Jessica Hoffmeyer
Chad and Misha Johns
Ruth Benedict
Dr. Dave and the Gordon Gang
Neil Mayo
Ryne and Samantha Swann
Jenah, Jermiah and Nathanael from KidsServe.com
Clark and Mary Kay Shepherd of A.C.T.S. Allowing Christ to Shine ministry
Joe Koenig and the Three Avocados: A Non Profit Coffee Company team
Todd and Vonda Hellner
Bryan Burt
Troy Bulson and family
Josh Wax
Jarod and Lani Hofacket
Gregg and Krista Murry
Steve and Debbie Chisolm
Chris McGurk
Alvin and Debbie Wade
Joey and Laura Tyson
Kayla Vance
Scott Lee
Byron Broten
Bevan and Laura Harms
Tim and Melissa Benedict
Jessie and Keisha Hagan

Emma Clarke
Leon and Kim Verriere
Sam Smith
Adam Drake
Steve and Jackie Roese
Helga Proudfoot
Christina and Amy Price

I believe South Sudan matters and I care deeply about the people there. Want to know why? Join the conversation at **southsudanmatters.com**.

A special thank-you to Daniel White and Food for the Hungry for joining me in the mission to introduce the Church to the beautiful people of South Sudan.

I would love to join your group as storyteller, teacher or Road to Becoming guide. For more information, please visit my website **www.jennysimmons.com**